Embellish Chic

Embellish
Chic

Detailing
Ready-to-Wear

Connie Long

The Taunton Press

The Taunton Press, Inc.
63 South Main Street, PO Box 5506
Newtown, CT 06470-5506
e-mail: tp@taunton.com

Distributed by Publishers Group West

Cover designer: Ann Marie Manca
Interior designer: Carol Petro
Layout artist: Carol Petro
Illustrator: Rosalie Vaccaro
Photographers: Jack Deutsch and Scott Phillips

Library of Congress Cataloging-in-Publication Data
Long, Connie.
    Embellish chic : detailing ready-to-wear / Connie Long.
            p. cm.
Includes index.
    ISBN 1-56158-485-1
 1. Fancy work. 2. Clothing and dress. I. Title.
    TT750 .L65 2002
    746.4--dc21   2002000359

Printed in the United States of America
10 9 8 7 6 5 4 3 2 1

The following manufacturers/brand names appearing
in *Embellish Chic* have trademarks: Armani®, Clover®,
Fusi-Knit™, Laura Ashley®, Nymo®, Pearls 'N Piping™,
Rit®, Stretch Magic Cord™, Sulky®, Teflon®, Tintex™,
Ultrasuede®, and Wonder-Under®.

To Ron, my husband and best friend,
whose wild sense of humor still makes me laugh
after all these years

Acknowledgments

My thanks to Sarah Coe for coming up with
the idea for this book and for offering me a chance
to develop it, and to Carol Spier for coming into
the project with a fresh approach that makes
all the elements work.

Contents

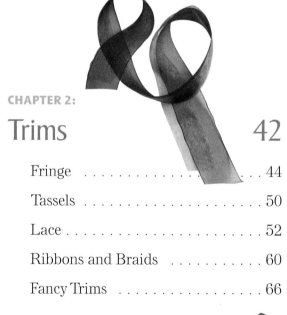

CHAPTER 2:

Trims   42

Introduction   2

CHAPTER 1:

Beads, Sequins & Buttons   6

Introduction

What fun it is to live in an age of embellishment. Everywhere I look at clothing—in department stores, boutiques, catalogs, fashion magazines, and on the street—I see beads and sequins, tassels and fringes, bright metallic studs, ribbons and braids, and embroidery both elegant and witty. Casual garb, party clothes, office attire—all manner of garments seem to be trimmed out in styles reminiscent of many historic periods, with diverse ethnic inspirations. Some of these clothes are beyond the reach of my pocketbook; some are one-of-a-kind and not available to me. And I can't generally find a source for those I admire in films or on television.

Yet when I turn my eyes in other directions, I see shelves stocked with plain denim jeans and jackets, T-shirts of all cuts and colors, and unadorned sweats. And there is rack upon rack of simple black dresses and basic one-color skirts and trousers, all perfectly serviceable and ubiquitously dull. But what an opportunity this set of clothing presents: the perfect canvas for my creativity. I can embellish these garments myself, have fun, create great-looking clothes, and know I've found an antidote to high-fashion price tags and unknown sources. And you can do the same.

Imagination is the key

"I don't know how to sew," you may say. That really doesn't matter. Many embellishments are simple additions of ready-made trim. When you want to dress up a plain garment, what you really need is inspiration and imagination—an idea for the way to enhance that plain T or too-basic sheath. In this book, I'll share lots of ideas with you, and you'll find others in the same places I do: the street, the shops, and the media.

You may never have sewn more than a button, but once you browse the pages of this book, you'll realize there are all manner of embellishments you can create with very simple sewing techniques; you'll even see that there are trims you can add without ever threading a needle. Of course, I do sew, and I'm sure some of you do as well, so there are also ideas here that require a sewing machine or are a bit more challenging. Additionally, if you do sew clothing, these embellishing techniques can enhance your from-scratch garments as well as the ready-to-wear clothes you purchase.

Embellish Chic

I knew when I created this book that every reader would have different garments to decorate. I wanted to be sure each of you would be able to do whatever strikes your fancy and not be limited to copying exactly some trimming that I created. So this is a book of embellishing techniques, not a book of projects. You'll see many photos of garments that I embellished, with captions explaining how I achieved that look; I hope you'll find these examples inspirational as well as informative. There are lots of step-by-step directions, many with photographs, that explain, for instance, how to sew on beads and sequins or different ways to add lace to a garment. There are no patterns for arranging the beads, sequins, or lace but myriad suggestions for how you can arrange them. You can use the directions and suggestions to sew beads

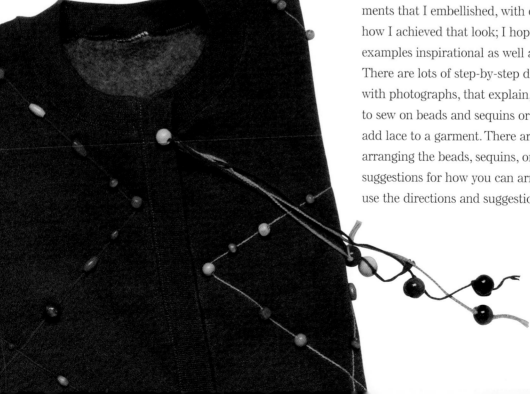

and sequins to any garment you like or to add lace to anything from a robe to a scarf.

In addition to the dozens of embellishment techniques with their step-by-step directions, you'll find sidebars that offer general information on embellishment materials. Some of these sidebars will help you understand which materials to use or purchase for specific types of embellishment; others give in-depth information on a method of work that can be applied to a variety of decorative techniques.

The more I worked on this book, the more inspirational ideas I realized I had to share with you. I have so many ideas for ways to use the various materials and techniques, there was no way I could possibly make samples of them all. Instead, you'll find these additional inspirations described in the Design Idea boxes that accompany many of the embellishment directions. Also, I developed several tricks for making the embellishment process faster, easier, and more fun; you'll find my tips for doing this sprinkled throughout the book.

Each of the five chapters is devoted to a different type of embellishment material. Chapter 1 explains how to work with beads, sequins, and buttons. Chapter 2 presents the wonderful world of purchased trims: ribbons, braids, ready-made fringe, and lace. Chapter 3 discusses fabric embellishments—using scraps, yardage, and vintage linens to make appliqués, borders, and unusual collages. Chapter 4 covers hardware: zippers, studs, nail heads, and the like; there are lots of no-sew techniques here. And Chapter 5 is devoted to embellishments made with threads of all weights.

So take out your plain clothes, make a trip to the trimmings store, and keep your mind open to the wonderful embellishment possibilities you see in the shops, on the street, and in this book. Then get started.

Beads, Sequins & Buttons

You can use bead and button embellishments to enhance virtually any part of garments, accessories, or home furnishings. Beads, sequins, and buttons come in many shapes and finishes, all of which are available singly or loose in small put-ups. Beads and sequins are also available as ready-made trim, as fringe, and as tassels.

The best way to apply individual beads, sequins, and buttons is by hand. Depending upon the effect you want to create, you can simply sew them on one at a time, or use one of the many specialty stitches explained in this chapter. Ready-made trims and fringes made of strung beads, pearls, or sequins can be sewn on by machine. Depending upon the structure of the trim and the effect desired, you'll sometimes need a special foot for your machine; other times a regular zigzag or zipper foot will work.

Hand-Beading Techniques

You will need some basic supplies for any of the following stitches that you will use when applying beading. Your choices of needle, thread, and beads will depend on the fabric you're working with. Practice the stitches on scrap fabric until you understand how they work, then experiment to find out which combination of materials will work best for the garment at hand.

When buying hand-beading needles, sizes 10 and 13 come together in the same package. Use size 10 for most beads, but switch to size 13 when the 10 is too large to fit through the hole. When choosing thread, match the thread color to the fabric. If you have chosen transparent beads, use monofilament clear light or clear dark color. Nymo® is my first choice because it is easy to thread and sew with few tangles. Size A is finer and less wiry than B, C, and D. My preference is to use one strand of the thicker thread because it is easier to sew with one strand. Use the finer thread on delicate and lightweight fabrics.

An optional item you may want to use is the Clover® Petit Cut thread cutter. Many standard threaders are not fine enough to work with a beading needle's very narrow elongated eye, but the Petit Cut from Clover is.

MATERIALS

Thread, Nymo size A, B, C, or D or all-purpose 100% polyester
Beeswax
Hand-beading needles, sizes 10 and 13
Beads
Embroidery hoop

TIP *Select beads in weights that are compatible with the fabric. Beads that are too heavy or large for the fabric will cause puckers and affect the fabric's drape.*

DESIGNER IDEA

A nice way to apply individual beads or sequins and get lots of impact or coverage on the garment is to scatter the beads along a focal point such as the neckline and shoulder area, the hemline, the waistline, or the collar. The part of the garment you embellish should be at a flattering place on your body. Emphasizing the neckline flatters everyone and draws the eyes to your face. Don't embellish hemlines that fall at areas you would prefer to de-emphasize, such as the hips or the thighs.

TIP *Spotting (scattering the beads) is easy to do on ready-made garments. You don't have to cut the thread between each bead position unless the beads are more than 2 in. apart, the garment is sheer, or the garment is close fitting and must stretch over the body.*

Running stitch

When filling or outlining an area, you can stitch beads in place either one or several at a time using a simple running stitch. Try this method with round

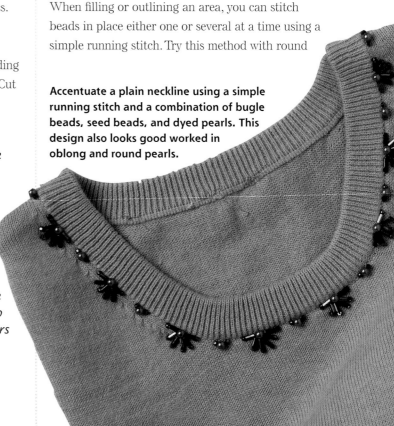

Accentuate a plain neckline using a simple running stitch and a combination of bugle beads, seed beads, and dyed pearls. This design also looks good worked in oblong and round pearls.

WORKING BY HAND

It is easy to apply beads and sequins by hand—difficulty isn't the issue. The big factor is time. If you choose a design that has a dense coverage of beads or sequins over a large part of the garment, it will take more time but not necessarily more skill to complete the project. Here are some basic decorative ways you can arrange beads and sequins when you are applying them by hand. The way you choose to combine materials will create further variations on these effects, so experiment.

Spotting. Arrange beads or sequins individually or in small clusters to accent the fabric. Sprinkle them randomly or highlight specific parts of a print or lace.

Outlining. Apply beads or sequins in a straight row or follow the outline of a motif. Sequins, bugle beads, and other oblong beads look best when applied individually, but round beads can be applied several at a time. In all cases, allow some space between the beads to keep the work from getting stiff. To sew rows of beads right next to each other, see "Couching" on p. 12.

Filling. Sew on several beads at a time using a running stitch to fill or cover an area. (When used this way, the running stitch is also called a satin stitch.) Sequins can also be used for filling.

Looping. Apply beads to form individual loops or clusters that are three-dimensional. You can use clusters of loops to accent motifs or form three-dimensional flowers.

Edging. Use beads or sequins to accentuate the edge of a garment. They can be close together or have a space between them. You can also apply beads so they extend beyond the edge to form a scallop or picot edge.

Fringe and tassels. If you make your own fringe and tassels, you can select the perfect beads to use. You can make the fringe directly on a garment or sew it to a tape first. Use fringe at any edge, but be aware of its weight and watch for the "droop" factor. Tassels are great for corners, belt ends, and to ornament dressmaker details such as tabs (see pp. 22–31 for specific ideas).

Why Work by Hand?

Whether you are applying beads or sequins, you'll find that:

- Hand techniques are the most versatile and offer the most options for attaching individual or multiple beads to ready-made garments.

- You have easier access to all parts of a garment when you sew by hand than by machine and more flexibility about how and where you place the beads.

- Hand beading is the easiest way to apply individual or groups of beads. It probably takes less time to apply individual beads by hand than it does by machine. In addition, hand sewing is less contrived to do and looks better and more finished.

- Hand-beading techniques are preferable on delicate or soft silks and chiffons because the hand-sewing stitches do not stress the fabric, and you can keep the work from getting stiff by allowing some space between the beads.

- You are less likely to need additional stabilizer because hand stitches don't put as much tension on the fabric as machine stitches do.

- Hand finishes give the look of fine quality to clothing.

WORKING WITH BEADS

You can buy basic beads loose, which are packaged by weight in tubes or bags, or on strings in hanks. A hank consists of 8 to 12 strings of beads. Loose beads are fine if you are sewing or arranging the beads one, two, or three at a time, but if you are couching, making fringe, or using a satin stitch, then you will save a lot of time by purchasing beads in hanks.

It is faster and easier to work with the beads if you leave them on their original string because the beads are all lined up and easily slide from their string over your needle. Separate one string from the hank by pulling the holding thread gently away from the other strands. Knot one end and pin or tape the knotted end to your work surface. By doing this, you can pull the unknotted end taut and insert your beading needle through the beads while they are still strung and slide the beads directly onto your beading needle. To see if the number of beads you have transferred is correct for your application, measure them while they are on the beading needle by holding them up against a ruler or marked guide.

or oblong beads such as seed beads, pearls, and bugle beads.

1. If you have chosen 100% polyester thread, use beeswax to further strengthen the thread and facilitate its passage through the fabric. After threading the needle, draw the thread across the beeswax once or twice, then press the thread with a dry iron at low temperature to smooth the surface for easy, tangle-free sewing.

2. Knot one end of the thread, and bring the needle up to the right side of the fabric and through one or more beads.

3. Bring the needle down to the wrong side of the fabric or garment next to the bead. For the bead or beads to lie flat, the stitch should be slightly longer than the beads (see the illustration on the facing page). If it is shorter, the beads will pucker away from the fabric.

Backstitch

The backstitch is best for spotting or sprinkling beads about randomly on the fabric and may be used to apply one or more beads per stitch. Use round or oblong beads such as seed beads, pearls, and bugle beads.

1. Wax the thread with beeswax if desired, and knot one end. Bring the needle up to the right side of the fabric and through one or more beads.

2. Bring the needle down to the wrong side of the fabric and to the right of the bead, then bring the needle up to the right side of the fabric and to the left of the first bead (see the illustration on the facing page).

Picot edge

The picot stitch accentuates necklines and edges by causing the beads to form a tiny zigzag edging. It works best with round or square beads rather than oblong ones. You can use a single color and type of bead, or use different colors and types to set off the outer bead that forms the picot point.

1. Sewing from right to left, knot one end of the thread and bring the needle up to the right side along the edge of the garment and through three beads. The first and third beads are called base beads because they will be in a row next to the fabric, whereas the second bead is the outer bead that will form a picot edge and stand away from the garment. Take a short stitch equal to the length of two beads through from the back of the fabric and along the edge.

2. For each following repeat, go up through the last base bead again and string two beads, an outer and a base bead. Take a short stitch equal to the length of two beads through from the back of the fabric (see the illustration on the facing page).

DESIGNER IDEA

By applying several beads per stitch and taking a stitch that is shorter than the length of beads, you can create interesting raised stitches that add texture.

Fence stitch

The fence stitch adds a spiky, three-dimensional effect to any area of the garment. Use bugle beads, seed beads, or small pearls.

1. Knot one end of the thread, and bring the needle up to the right side of the fabric and through three beads, a bugle bead, a seed bead, and a second bugle bead in that order. Take a short stitch through to the back of the fabric.

2. Take the next stitch through to the right side of the fabric next to the previous stitch (see the illustration at right).

RUNNING STITCH

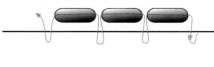

BACKSTITCH

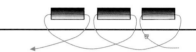

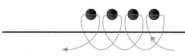

PICOT EDGE

FENCE STITCH

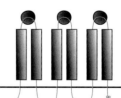

A hand-beaded, simple picot edging dresses up the neckline and armholes of this printed silk georgette dress. The ends of the belt sparkle with a delicate fringe made from the same beads.

FENCE STITCH VARIATION

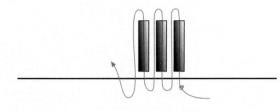

LOOP STITCH

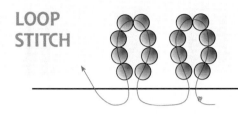

SINGLE-NEEDLE COUCHING

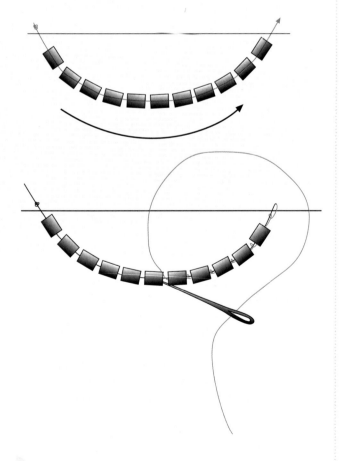

Loop stitch

The loop stitch stands away from the garment and is a wonderful stitch to use when you want to accent or add texture to an area of your design. Choose small beads, round or square; you can use all of the same type or combine different beads.

1. Knot one end of the thread, and bring the needle up to the right side of the fabric and through several small beads (five or more).

2. Take a very short stitch to bring the needle down through to the wrong side of the fabric.

3. Repeat next to or a distance away from the first loop (see the illustration at left).

Couching

Couching is a good and relatively fast way to apply strings of beads very close together in straight or curved lines and around corners. Instead of passing through each bead, the couching stitch is worked over the thread on which the beads are strung. Oblong, round, and square beads all couch nicely. You can couch bugles, seed beads, pearls, and novelty beads instead of sewing them individually when you want the beads to closely butt together on the design. There are two couching techniques—single needle and double needle. Use single-needle couching (also known as closed-ended couching) for distances of less than 4 in. and double-needle couching (also called open-ended couching) for long distances, such as along a neckline, hemline, or within the garment.

Single-needle couching

1. Knot one end of the thread, and bring the needle up to the right side of the fabric.

2. Thread the number of beads it takes to cover the length of the design line, checking this by laying the beads along your design (see the illustration on the facing page).

3. Bring the needle down to the wrong side of the fabric, then sew a tiny backstitch or a tailor's knot to fasten the holding thread.

4. Next, start couching the holding thread. Do this by bringing the same needle up to the right side of the fabric between two beads and taking a very short stitch over the holding thread and back to the wrong side of the fabric. Repeat at even intervals, every three or more beads when using small beads such as seed beads. Bugles and other oblong beads look best if you secure between all adjacent beads (see the illustration on the facing page).

5. When you get back to where you started, secure the thread on the wrong side by forming three tailor's knots under the end bead.

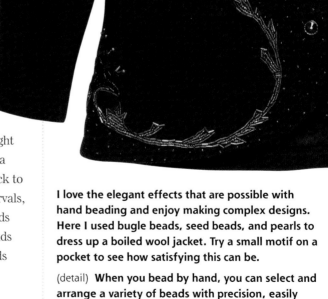

I love the elegant effects that are possible with hand beading and enjoy making complex designs. Here I used bugle beads, seed beads, and pearls to dress up a boiled wool jacket. Try a small motif on a pocket to see how satisfying this can be.

(detail) When you bead by hand, you can select and arrange a variety of beads with precision, easily and efficiently spacing them exactly as you wish.

DESIGNER IDEA

Use single-needle couching to outline a small area of your design such as the stem of a flower or leaf and to fill in that flower and leaf if you want them to be completely flat on the garment. Otherwise, combine techniques by using couching for just the stems and a satin stitch to fill in. The second option is a little faster, and the beads will bow away from the fabric slightly.

Double-needle couching

When double-needle couching, you will be working with a hank of strung beads. This consists of 8 to 12 strings, with each string typically ranging in length from 16 in. to 20 in. A string is also called a loop because each string is folded in half on the hank. Typically the string in a purchased hank is not of good quality, so normally you should restring the beads as you work.

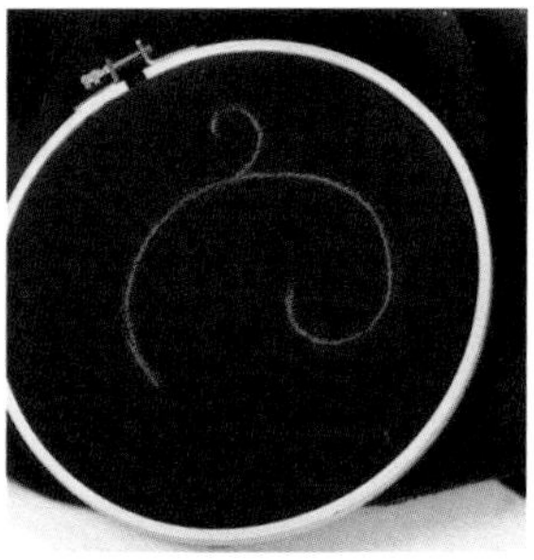

1. Using an embroidery hoop, frame the area you are beading.

2. Cut a piece of thread about 30 in. long, then knot one end of the thread and bring the needle up to the right side of the fabric. Also sew a tailor's knot in place.

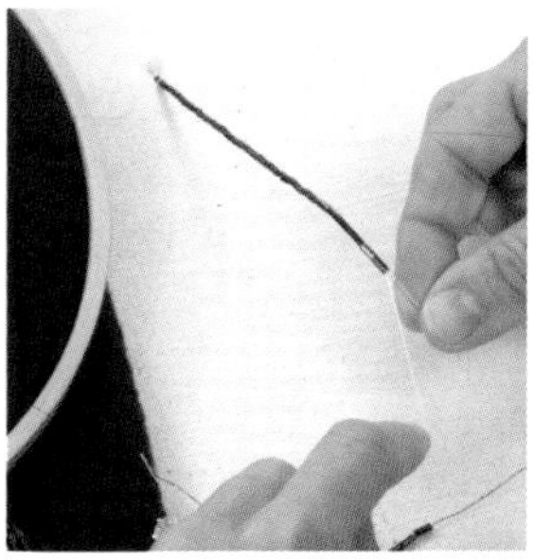

3. Transfer the prestrung beads to the thread by inserting the beading needle through as many beads as possible. You will be able to slide the beads from the string, over your needle, and onto the new (and better-quality) thread.

4. Remove the beading needle, but tie a big, clumpy knot at the end of the thread to prevent the beads from sliding off the holding thread. Tie the knot about 8 in. away from the last bead.

5. Next, thread a beading needle with a new thread and knot one end. Then bring the needle up to the right side of the fabric and through the first bead to sew it in place conventionally (through the hole).

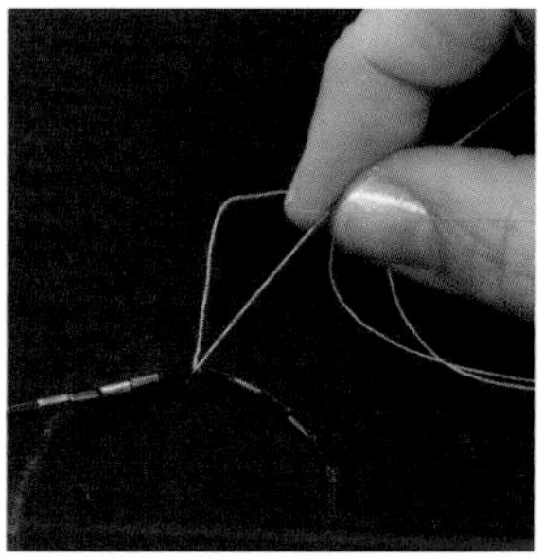

6. Slide one bead or more next to the first bead and couch over the holding thread. Continue this way until all beads have been couched into position or you've reached the end of the design. It is important to stop couching with enough thread left on your couching needle to be able to sew several stitches into the fabric.

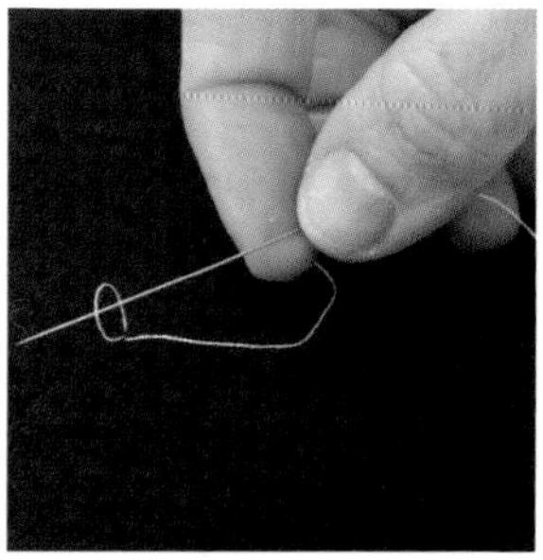

7. Remove any extra beads from the holding thread. Using a regular or beading needle, secure the holding thread by bringing it to the wrong side of the fabric and sewing three tailor's knots in place.

If the beads you are using are strung onto good-quality nylon thread, there is no reason to restring them. In this case, start by tying a knot at one end of the thread to keep the beads from falling off while you work. Thread the other end onto a fine crewel needle (about a size 8 or

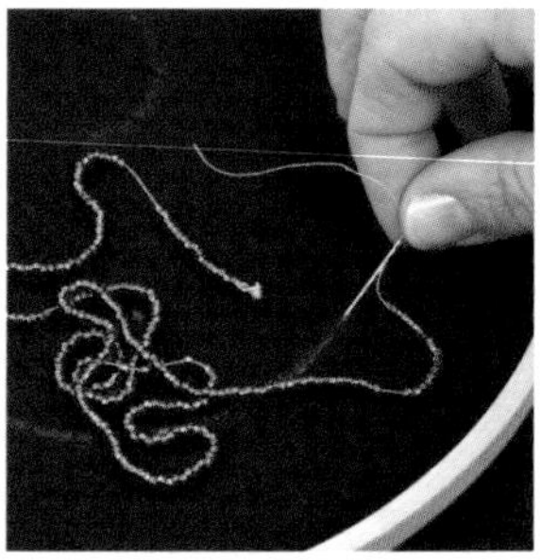

DESIGNER **IDEA**

Use double-needle couching to create beaded curlicues or squiggles within the garment or along collars and edges. You can also use it to define seamlines, particularly princess seams or darts, but you won't be able to frame shaped areas, so choose this effect if your fabric is firm.

the finest needle that will fit the thread without damaging the fabric). Holding the beads on the right side of your garment, pass the needle through to the wrong side at the point where you want the couched design to begin. Secure the string using three tailor's knots.

Applying Sequins by Hand

Sequins come in several styles and finishes—they can be flat or cupped (faceted), matte or shiny. Generally they have a hole, or eye, in the center, but sometimes the eye is placed closer to the edge, in which case they are called *paillettes*. They are available in a variety of sizes and of course in myriad colors. The different types create different looks, and when combined, they create nearly limitless decorative effects.

You will need some basic supplies for any of the following stitches that you will use when applying sequins. Your choices of needle, thread, and sequins will depend on the fabric you're working with and the technique you are using. Practice the stitches on scrap fabric until you understand how they work, then experiment to find out which combination of materials will work best for the garment at hand.

Most of the general rules for applying beads by hand are true as well for sequins, so read the section "Working with Beads" on p. 10.

HAND-COUCHING GUIDELINES

- When adding a couched embellishment to ready-to-wear (or any finished garment), place it on firm (interfaced) areas of the garment or on an area that can be framed in a hoop.

- Lines of hand-couched beads are a bit stiffer than lines of individually sewn beads but are more pliable than machine-couched beads.

- When hand couching, you can place one line of beads next to another and have lines of beads intersect or cross one another.

- Couching is not suitable for use on areas that need to stretch or be soft.

MATERIALS

Embroidery hoop
Thread, all-purpose 100% polyester or monofilament
Needle, all-purpose sharp or crewel size 9
Sequins

Invisible sequin stitch/ overlapped sequins

Overlapped sequins create a dramatic fish-scale effect that really brings out the design, especially when you apply the sequins following curves and turning corners. To catch the light and enhance the design further, change the direction of the overlap (even if the sequins are matte).

1. When possible, frame the fabric in an embroidery hoop. For the first sequin only, knot one end of the thread and bring the needle up from the wrong to the right side of the fabric and from back to front through the eye of the first sequin.

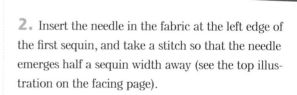

A combination of flat and cupped gold sequins, applied using the invisible sequin/overlap sequin, backstitch/flat sequin, and beads with sequins techniques, enhances the abstract paisleys printed on this scarf. Each motif reflects the light a little differently.

(detail) **There are many ways to bead the same design by using a single type and size of bead or sequin or an assortment. The effect will be different if you choose beads that match the background color, if they are all the same contrasting color, or if they are a variety of colors.**

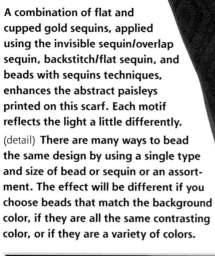

2. Insert the needle in the fabric at the left edge of the first sequin, and take a stitch so that the needle emerges half a sequin width away (see the top illustration on the facing page).

3. Pick up a new sequin by inserting the needle from front to back through the eye, then insert the needle in the fabric again at the left edge of the previous sequin. Take another stitch, bringing the needle out a full sequin width away this time. When you pull the thread taut, the right half of the second sequin will overlap the first sequin.

4. Repeat step 3 as often as desired. To end, bring the needle to the wrong side of the fabric at the left edge of the last sequin, and secure the thread using three tailor's knots behind the last sequin (see the top illustration on the facing page).

Backstitch/flat sequin application

By using a backstitch, you can place sequins next to one another or up to 2 in. apart. This stitch keeps the sequins flat on the fabric so they do not flip or move out of position. Monofilament thread blends best here since you see the thread across the surface of the sequin. Otherwise match the thread color to the sequin color.

1. Knot one end of the thread, and bring the needle up from the wrong side to the right side of the garment and through the eye of the first sequin.

2. To work the backstitch, insert the needle to the right of the sequin, bring it up again to the left of the sequin, then insert it through the eye and bring it out on the back of the garment.

3. Bring the needle up to the right side of the fabric where you would like the center of the next sequin to be, and thread the eye of the next sequin onto it (see the illustration at right).

4. Repeat steps 2 and 3.

Transparent, flat sequins add a wash of color to the embroidered flowers on this silk georgette scarf. I applied the sequins individually to the petals using the beads with sequins and backstitch/ flat sequin stitches.

INVISIBLE OR OVERLAPPED SEQUIN APPLICATION

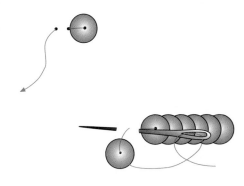

BACKSTITCH/ FLAT SEQUIN APPLICATION

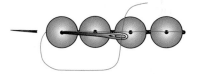

BEADS WITH SEQUINS APPLICATION

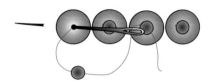

OPTIONAL CENTERS

Loop in the center

*Bugle and bead
in the center*

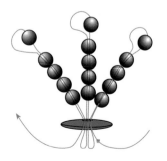

Tassel in the center

Beads with sequins

The following technique uses one or more beads to hold each sequin in place and has a three-dimensional effect. You can place the sequins next to each other or up to 2 in. apart.

1. Knot one end of the thread, and bring the needle up from the wrong side to the right side of the fabric; pass it through the eye of the first sequin and through one small bead.

2. Pass the needle back through the eye of the sequin to the wrong side of the fabric. Pull tightly so the bead rests firmly and holds the sequin in place.

3. Bring the needle up to the right side of the fabric where you would like the center of the next sequin to be, and thread the next sequin and bead onto it (see the top illustration at left).

4. Repeat steps 2 and 3.

TIP *Sequins applied using either the flat sequin application or the beads with sequins application are low maintenance because the sequins stay in place without flipping away from the garment. This is especially important on casual clothes, T-shirts, and any garment that you plan to wash.*

Sequin squiggles

To cover larger areas and fill in motifs with sequins, use sequin trim and couch it in place by hand. Sequin trim is flexible and easy to sew invisibly because the sequins overlap. First outline a design motif or area on your garment, then just squiggle the trim back and forth across the line, couching it at various intervals. By doing this, you can quickly cover substantial areas.

In addition to sequin trim and your basic beading supplies, you will need a beading needle or size 9 standard needle (sharp) and a size 9 crewel needle.

1. Begin by marking the design area on your garment. It can be a closed motif, such as a paisley shape, or a straight, curved, or bent line. If you want to use this technique to parallel an edge, place the design line far enough inside the edge for you to be able to keep the squiggled sequins on the garment.

2. Pull the sequins off one end of the trim to create a tail about 4 in. long, which you'll fasten after you've finished couching. Position the trim across the design line, extending the tail  beyond the point where you want to begin couching.

3. Knot one end of the thread, and bring the needle up from the wrong side to the right side of the fabric next to the first sequin left on the trim. Take a stitch over the sequin trim, passing the needle to the wrong side of the fabric, then stitch over the trim again a short distance away.

4. Arrange the trim in a pattern that squiggles back and forth across the marked line, and stitch over the trim at whatever intervals are necessary to secure the squiggles.

FUN SEQUIN-BEAD COMBINATIONS

Here are several other ways you can fasten sequins with beads (see the illustrations on the facing page).

- **Loop in the center.** Thread more than one small bead onto the needle. When you pass the needle through the sequin again, the beads will form a small loop. Experiment to see how many beads give the effect you want.

- **Bugle and small bead in the center.** Thread one or more bugle beads onto the needle, then add one small seed bead. Pull the thread through, and pass the needle through the bugle beads again and through the sequin to the wrong side of the fabric.

- **Tassel in the center.** Thread three or more bugle beads onto the needle, then add one small seed bead. Pull the thread through, and pass the needle through the bugle beads again and through the sequin to the wrong side of the fabric. Repeat several times to create a tassel. You can also do this by using five or more seed beads instead of the bugle beads.

5. When you are finished couching, secure the thread using three tailor's knots on the wrong side of the fabric. Cut the thread, then cut off the extra sequin trim 4 in. beyond the couching.

6. Remove the sequins on the tail from their supporting threads, then use the crewel needle to pass the threads to the wrong side of the garment. Tie the threads together.

Buttons

To heavily embellish small areas of a garment such as collars, cuffs, or waistbands, or accessories such as belts, purse handles, and hat bands, you can stitch assorted buttons as close as possible to each other. Or arrange buttons to form a motif just as you would with beads. For quick embellishments, take advantage of the many shaped buttons—flowers and animals are just a few of the motifs you'll find—and arrange them to create a picture. Large, flat, sew-through buttons look great if you sew them in place

Sewing an assortment of buttons over the entire collar adds some color, texture, and fun to an otherwise prim or plain jacket.

using colorful embroidery threads that stand out as much as the buttons do, and they can add a pretty border to the edge of a garment.

Embellishing small areas

Heavily embellishing any area with buttons adds a lot of weight, even if you choose buttons that are extremely light. This technique is only appropriate for garment areas that have body, such as collars and cuffs, but not if they are made of something like silk chiffon, which is too soft and lightweight. Instead, think of using crisp shirt collars or, better still, crisp jacket collars. Then you can heavily encrust the area without having to change anything about the garment.

MATERIALS

Buttons in assorted sizes, shapes, and colors
Thread, all-purpose 100% polyester or
buttonhole twist in a color that matches the
garment fabric
Needle, sharp or crewel, size 8, 9, or whatever's
appropriate for fabric

1. Start by positioning and sewing the more interesting or special buttons. By doing this, you can place the ones you like best in areas where you are more likely to notice them  first and enjoy them, such as near the front points of a collar or center of a neckline. You can also distribute the prettier buttons evenly and fill in with plain ones.

2. Thread the needle, then double and knot the thread. To better support the buttons, sew through all of the collar layers even though the stitches will show on the underside of the collar. Sew through each button three or four times, then isolate the stitch by sewing a tailor's knot on the back of the collar. Insert the needle between the fabric layer to emerge at the next button placement.

3. Bring the thread out to the top of the collar, isolate the stitch again using a tailor's knot, and begin sewing the next button.

4. Repeat the process until the entire collar is covered.

Large, flat, sew-through buttons

Flat, plain, sew-through buttons look like huge sequins when you sew them in place using pretty threads. Position the buttons in a row along hems and edges or following seams. These buttons look best if there is some space between them.

To sew four-hole buttons with some added zip, try sewing them so the thread forms an X between the holes and the edge but not in the center. You can sew two-hole buttons in a similar way, with the thread going from the buttonholes, over the edge of the button, and into the material. Use decorative threads such as embroidery floss, pearl cotton, fine ribbon, or raffia to sew the buttons to the garment.

Beading Fringe by Hand

Beaded fringe adds instant glamour to any project. It is important to consider the droop factor when you choose to use handmade or ready-made beaded fringe. Make sure the weight of the fringe works with the weight of the fabric, particularly when the placement is along an upper edge, such as along the top of a pocket, a wide neckline, a lapel, or a collar. Droop is not an issue on standard hemlines because the hemline and the fringe hang parallel to the floor, but heavy fringe might distort a bias hemline.

You can bead fringe directly onto the edge of a garment or, by beading onto a piece of ribbon or twill tape, create a fringed trim to sew on. Once you understand the basic concept, you can come up with all sorts of wonderful variations of your own. An advantage to making fringed trim is that if you tire of the garment, you can remove and reuse the trim.

If you make fringed trim, you can sew the ribbon or tape on by hand or machine (see pp. 44–45 for machine-sewing directions).

TIP *Although dangling strands of beads are susceptible to damage, typically from snagging onto other things, they are otherwise pretty resilient. Whether handmade or ready-made, most beaded trims are wash-able, so you can use them on a wide range of items including clothing, accessories, and home furnishings. These trims look as fabu-lous on denim and T-shirts as they do on silk.*

Straight fringe

Basic beaded fringe is simple and effective, with straight, clean lines that you can play up or modify through your choice of beads. Using a single type of bead creates a string bean effect. To make fringe with long, fluid strands, use all-purpose polyester thread. To make fringe with short and stiff strands, use Nymo size D thread.

By deciding how deep (the measurement from top to bottom) you plan to make the fringe and how densely you will space the strands, you can get a good idea of how many beads to buy. For example, if your chosen beads come on 20-in.-long strings and you want to make 2-in.-deep fringe, you will get 10 strands of fringe from each string of beads. If you space five strands per inch along the garment edge, then each 20-in. string of beads will make enough 2-in.-deep fringe to edge 2 in. of the garment.

Your choice of thread depends on whether you want a fluid fringe or a stiff fringe. Long fringes and tassels look best when they are soft and fluid, but short fringes can be stiff and spiky if that is the look you're after. I prefer to use a single thread in the thickest size (for strength and durability) that gives the desired drape for the bead I am using, rather than a double length of a finer thread that gives the same

You can create a lively zigzag edge by using strands of graduated lengths to make a basic, straight beaded fringe.

drape. Naturally, fine beads need a finer thread (size A), but large or heavy beads can use a size D. A double length of Nymo size D will give you a stiff and spiky fringe if you use small, lightweight beads and keep the fringe depth less than 1 in.

MATERIALS

Thread, all-purpose 100% polyester or Nymo size A, B, C, or D
Beading needles, sizes 10 and 13
Ribbon or twill tape, optional
Hanks of beads, a single type and size or a variety
Pliers, optional

1. Decide on the depth of the fringe. To make the strands consistent, it is easier to use a mea-surement than to count beads. Either use a ruler, work on a gridded surface, or mark two parallel lines on a piece of paper to use as a measuring guide.

TIP *For fringe with a zigzag edge like that shown on the pants in the top photo, make an actual-size diagram showing the depth of each consecutive strand in one zigzag repeat.*

BASIC
BEADED FRINGE

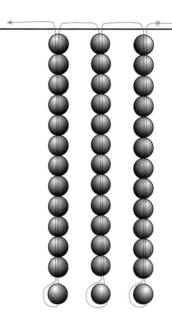

TIP *Small pliers are useful when stringing beads. Use them to break "wild" beads that are too small to fit past the eye of the needle. Break the problem bead while it is over the needle shaft so you can avoid having to restring the beads.*

2. Thread a beading needle (size 10 for most beads or size 13 for very small beads), and knot the thread when it is possible to hide the knot under a seam or behind the hem allowance. Otherwise start by sewing several tailor's knots on the wrong side of the ribbon or garment until the thread stops sliding.

3. Bring the needle out through the ribbon or garment where you want to start the fringe, and pass it through the length of beads you wish to use.

4. Go around the last bead, back through all the remaining beads, and then back into the ribbon or garment. Take a tiny stitch to lock the strand of fringe in place.

5. Next, insert the needle into the ribbon or garment and take a stitch so that the needle emerges where you want to place the next strand. A ½-in. distance between strands works well with a variety of beads, but you can decrease the space between each strand to create a dense fringe or increase the space between each strand to create a more open effect.

6. Repeat steps 3 through 5 as many times as necessary to fringe the garment edge or desired length of ribbon.

TIP *Don't go out on a limb! Every time you are about to repeat step 3, be sure you have enough thread to complete the entire fringe strand. Your thread should be long enough to allow you to get back to the fabric and tie it off.*

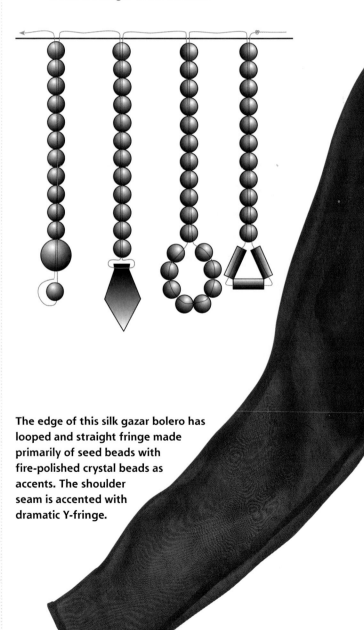

DESIGNER IDEA

Try attaching a deep, fluid fringe trim to the hemline of a short dress or skirt to create a pretty peek-a-boo effect when you walk.

You could also dress up a pillow by stitching a short, chunky beaded-fringe trim along the edge. The fringe will catch the changing light and add a play of color to the edge. If the fringe is on twill tape, cover the tape with a decorative braid or ribbon trim.

Making looped fringe

Basic looped fringe creates a pretty swagged edging that you can modify by changing the spacing, the number, and the types of beads. Change the spacing a little and the loop becomes a swag, a V, or a Y. All the variations spread the beads out more than in a straight fringe, so you get lots of coverage using fewer beads.

MATERIALS

Thread, Nymo size A, B, C, or D
Beading needle, size 10, 11, 12, or 13
Ribbon or twill tape, optional
Beads
Pliers, optional

1. Decide on the size of the loop—you need to calculate the length of thread needed for each loop and the interval at which the thread will be attached to the garment edge (be sure it repeats evenly along the edge). To make the thread length the same for each loop, it is easier to use a measurement than to count beads. Either use a ruler, work on a gridded surface, or mark two parallel lines on a piece of paper to use as a measuring guide.

2. Thread the beading needle and knot the thread when it is possible to hide the knot under a seam or behind the hem allowance. Otherwise start by sewing

FRINGE END IDEAS

Here are ways to make the end of each fringe strand special.

- Use a teardrop-shaped bead at the bottom of each strand.

- Use a large, special bead as the second from the bottom and a small, inconspicuous bead at the bottom.

- Create a small loop at the bottom.

- Create a triangle at the bottom.

The edge of this silk gazar bolero has looped and straight fringe made primarily of seed beads with fire-polished crystal beads as accents. The shoulder seam is accented with dramatic Y-fringe.

several tailor's knots in place on the wrong side of the ribbon or garment until the thread stops sliding.

3. Bring the needle out through the ribbon or garment where you want to start the fringe, and pass it through the depth of beads you wish to use.

4. Connect the other end to the ribbon or garment either next to or just to the left of the starting point to form a loop (see the illustration at right).

5. Isolate each repeat by doing a tailor's knot.

LOOPED FRINGE

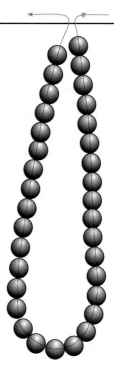

LOOP FRINGE VARIATIONS

Here are some other effects you can create by using looped fringe.

- Connect one end of the strung beads a distance away from the other to create a scalloped or swag effect.

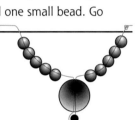

- Create a V by stringing enough beads to form half the swag, then going through one larger bead and one small bead. Go around the small bead, through the larger bead, then finish the second half of the swag.

- Create a Y fringe by stringing enough beads to form half the swag, then going through one different or marker bead, plus enough beads to form the leg of the Y. Go around the last bead and through the leg beads plus the marker bead. Then pass the needle through enough beads to complete the second half of the swag.

Beautiful beaded tassels are easy to make from beaded fringe— you can start with purchased fringe or make your own on a piece of ribbon.

Making branched fringe

Branched fringe has an appealing organic shape that can look like branches of coral, twigs, or icicles depending on the colors and finish of your beads. Because each branch has more volume than standard straight fringe, you use fewer strands of fringe and get lots of coverage. This fringe looks great at the top or bottom of a purse and at the edge of a scarf. Increase or decrease the depth of the fringe or increase the number of branches to vary the results.

MATERIALS

Thread, Nymo size A, B, C, or D
Beading needle, size 10, 11, 12, or 13
Ribbon or twill tape, optional
Seed beads or assorted small beads
Pliers, optional

1. Thread the beading needle and knot the thread when it is possible to hide the knot under a seam or

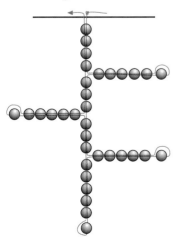

5. Repeat step 4 until you get near the top of the main branch, then go through the remaining beads and the fabric. For durability, secure each entire strand with a tailor's knot.

6. Repeat steps 2 through 5 as often as you'd like.

Beaded Tassels

Beaded tassels can accent closures, corners, and points on clothing, accessories, and home furnishings with the perfect finial. What sets beaded tassels apart from other tassels is the medium. Beaded tassels may sparkle, be transparent, frosted, iridescent, made out of wood, or have shell accents. They stimulate the senses and make a bold statement.

behind the hem allowance. Otherwise start by sewing several tailor's knots in place on the wrong side of the ribbon or garment until the thread stops sliding.

2. Bring the needle out through the fabric where you want to start the fringe, and pass it through a 2-in.-length of seed beads, which will be the "main" branch of the first strand of fringe.

3. Go around the last bead, pass the needle back through the next five beads only, and pull it through.

4. To add a "minor" branch, pick up six or more beads from your supply string or dish, pulling the needle through them. Go around the end bead and back through the five plus three more on the main branch.

Making tassels from beaded fringe

You can make beaded tassels by rolling up a length of fringed trim, then covering the header with a decorative trim or, better still, sewing individual beads or sequins to the header.

MATERIALS

Purchased or handmade beaded trim
Thread, 100% polyester
Beading needle, size 10, 11, 12, or 13
Fine cord or ribbon, 3 in. to 4 in. for each
   holding loop
Glue or double-sided tape, optional
Purchased braid, optional
Masking tape or liquid fray retardant, optional

1. If necessary, secure both ends of the fringe header so that the beads don't fall off while you're working. Use a straight stitch, a zigzag stitch, or overcast by hand, depending on which is more convenient.

2. To get an idea of how much fringe to use for one tassel, tightly roll the header until the fringe falls in a cluster of the desired density, then mark the cutoff point on the header.

Unroll the trim, stabilize the header on both sides of the mark, and cut. Unfasten any loose beads, and save them to cover the top of the tassel.

3. Place the trim on a flat surface with the header wrong side up (if there is a wrong side).

4. To make a hanging loop, cut a 3-in.- to 4-in.-long cord or narrow trim. Fold the cord in half to form a loop, then sew or glue both ends of the loop ½ in. away from one end of the fringe header with the cord ends extending into the fringe.

5. Roll the fringe header, starting at the loop end. If the starting end won't stay tight while you work, secure it using glue. Turn under and sew or glue the end of the header to hide the cut end.

TIP *If you've used glue, wait for it to dry before you hand-sew anything.*

6. Embellish the top of the tassel with purchased braid or by randomly sewing on individual beads to cover the exposed header. Most braids unravel easily when you cut them, making it difficult to finish the edge. Since you are just wrapping the trim around the top of the tassel, finish the starting end by covering it with a small piece of masking tape or coating it with liquid fray retardant. Finish the other end by machine- or hand-sewing to prevent raveling, then cut off any raveled excess next to the stitches. Turn under the stitched edge and slipstitch to the tassel. You can also cover a ribbon loop with tiny beads.

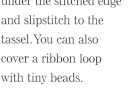

Making tassels from loose beads

You can make your own beaded tassels using a single type of bead or, better still, a variety of beads. Make them to coordinate with other beadwork on the garment or as unique accents. The larger the bead you use for the top, the more dramatic the tassel will be.

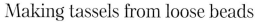

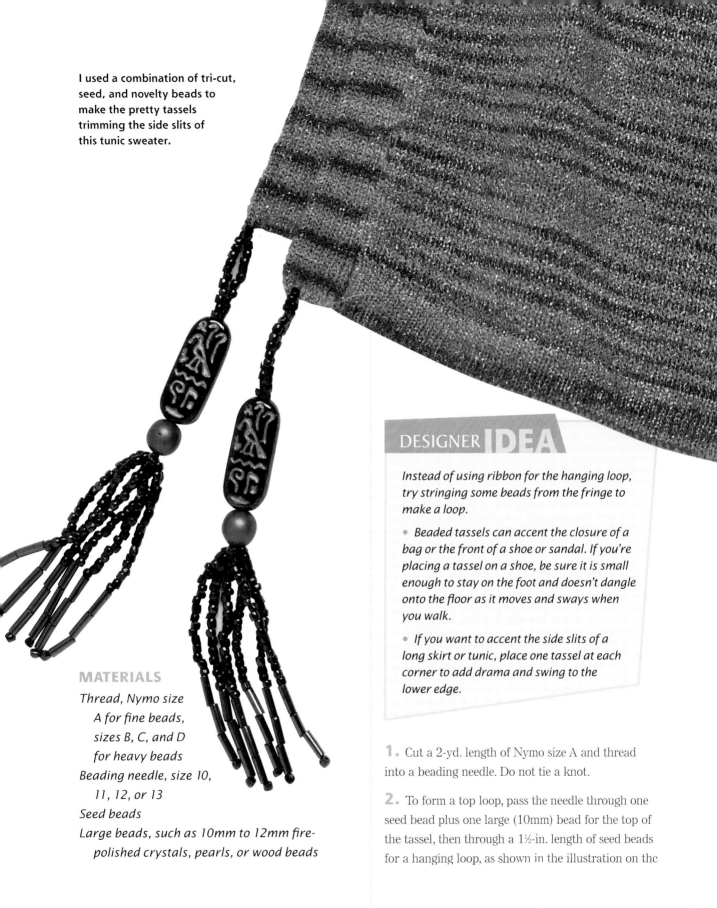

I used a combination of tri-cut, seed, and novelty beads to make the pretty tassels trimming the side slits of this tunic sweater.

MATERIALS

Thread, Nymo size A for fine beads, sizes B, C, and D for heavy beads
Beading needle, size 10, 11, 12, or 13
Seed beads
Large beads, such as 10mm to 12mm fire-polished crystals, pearls, or wood beads

DESIGNER IDEA

Instead of using ribbon for the hanging loop, try stringing some beads from the fringe to make a loop.

• *Beaded tassels can accent the closure of a bag or the front of a shoe or sandal. If you're placing a tassel on a shoe, be sure it is small enough to stay on the foot and doesn't dangle onto the floor as it moves and sways when you walk.*

• *If you want to accent the side slits of a long skirt or tunic, place one tassel at each corner to add drama and swing to the lower edge.*

1. Cut a 2-yd. length of Nymo size A and thread into a beading needle. Do not tie a knot.

2. To form a top loop, pass the needle through one seed bead plus one large (10mm) bead for the top of the tassel, then through a 1½-in. length of seed beads for a hanging loop, as shown in the illustration on the facing page. (The initial seed bead acts as a stopper when you tie the threads to form the holding loop.)

3. Bring the needle back through the large bead but not through the first seed bead. Next, bring the cut ends of the thread together without removing the needle and slide all the beads along the thread so

that they are centered on the thread and a loop forms above the large bead. Tie the threads together below the large bead and next to the first seed bead to hold the loop in place; do not cut the thread.

4. Start the first strand of fringe by passing the needle through a 2-in. length of beads, around the last bead, and back through the remaining beads, bringing it out between the seed bead stopper and the topper. Tie the active thread (with the beading needle) to the inactive remaining thread.

5. Repeat step 4 to make additional strands of fringe. You will be able to make six strands with the active half of the thread.

6. To end, tie the active thread to the inactive thread, then pass the needle through the large topper bead, through the loop, and through the topper bead

DESIGNER IDEA

You can make a single, beautiful beaded tassel to slide onto a necklace. Either keep the tassel neutral to match the chain by using silver or gold beads, or go wild with color and all different kinds of beads. Or make a variety of tassels using different bead combinations to wear with different outfits.

Try adding beaded tassels to other items such as to the top of a decorative box or to each end of a table runner. When buying beads, bring the box or runner with you so that you select beads that bring out its best features.

Test couching techniques on a fabric similar to the garment fabric. You can eliminate puckers next to the beads by loosening the needle tension and by adding stabilizer to the back of the design field.

again. Tie the thread again, pass the remaining end through one strand of the fringe, and cut off the excess thread.

7. Use the inactive thread to make more fringe if you wish, or pass it through one strand of fringe and cut off the excess.

Machine-Couching Techniques

Beaded trims are firm and dense. The best applications for them feature straight lines, curved lines, swirls, or simple shapes. To avoid overpowering a garment, limit them to outlines, borders, and isolated motifs. Sequin trim is more flexible and flatter than beaded trim, so you can easily sew swirls, zigzag patterns, and other designs where the sequin trim turns sharply or crosses over other rows of trim.

If possible, place the portion of the garment you are embellishing in an embroidery hoop. If not, frame the area with your hands while couching.

Take the time to experiment on a scrap of fabric so you can get the hang of the process. Try to find a scrap with a similar weight and drape to your garment's fabric, especially if the garment is lightweight. This way you will learn whether or not interfacing is needed. To practice, first read the directions for each technique all the way through because you'll see the stitches for beginning and ending are not the same as for sewing on the length of trim. Then draw the shape you think you want to embellish on scrap fabric and try beading over it to learn if it is possible or whether you need to modify the shape of the design. Always test the presser foot with your trim so that you learn its limitations.

When using cross-locked glass beads or any beaded or sequined trim assembled with threads, allow several inches of trim to extend at each end. Leave a short extension when using molded trim; you need just enough to be able to grab the trim behind

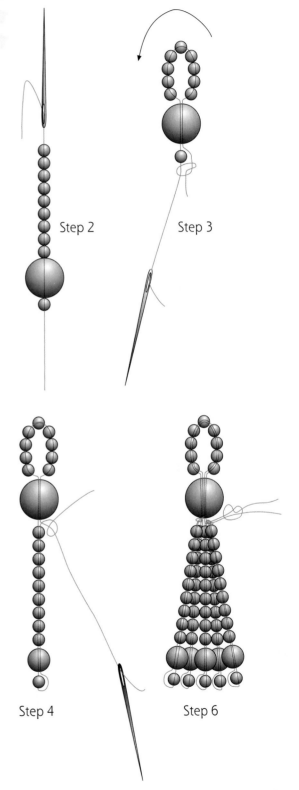

Step 2

Step 3

Step 4

Step 6

WORKING BY MACHINE

Although the only hand-beading technique that can be replaced by machine is double-needle couching, the possible effects you can achieve when couching by machine are diverse, attractive, and, unlike hand couching, extra quick to do. Machine application is appropriate, easy, and surprisingly versatile when you are using beaded trim, sequined trim, or individual beads that you've strung onto a holding thread. The latter has infinite variations.

What Can the Machine Do?

Here are some considerations and guidelines for sewing on beads or sequins by machine.

- Start with beads that are already on a string or sewn together to form a trim, such as cross-locked beads, molded pearl and bead trim, and sequin trim. You can use loose beads if you first string them onto a transparent or decorative

holding thread. The size of the beads or pearls must not exceed the width of your zigzag (4mm to 5mm is the widest setting for most machines).

- Machine-couched beaded trims are stiffer than hand-couched strung beads. Use them on garments made from fabrics with good body, such as tapestry, denim, raw silk, bottom-weight cottons, and sweatshirt knits, and in areas of the garment that benefit from the added stiffness of the trim, such as collars, waistlines, the edges of a jacket, and hemlines.

- Loose beads that you string onto a holding cord and then couch by machine are less stiff than couched trim because you create space between the individual beads.

- To machine-bead on a single layer of a garment, add stabilizer behind the area you will be embellishing (see the sidebar on p. 75), frame it in a hoop, then remove the excess stabilizer after stitching.

the presser foot. When you begin to sew, always pull approximately 8 in. of thread from both the needle and the bobbin so that when you are done you can pull it through to the wrong side and tie a knot.

Couching beaded trim by machine

Cross-locked beads and 2mm pearl or beaded trims are more flexible than larger beads, so they conform more easily to a garment and to curved design lines. Because these trims are not bulky, you can run one line of trim across another without interrupting the trim or the stitching, but at intersections you must manually turn the handwheel of the machine to avoid breaking the needle.

For both esthetic and logistical reasons, machine-couched beaded trims are perfect for garment edges, necklines, hems on pants, dresses, skirts, tops, and sleeves, and collars and cuffs. These areas are easier to access with a sewing machine than are interior areas on a ready-made garment, and they also have the extra body that will make your sewing go smoothly without the need for additional stabilizer.

Interior areas of the garment typically need stabilizing; obvious puckers next to the couched beads of your test sample tell you to use interfacing. I like to use lightweight fusible tricot (my favorite is So Sheer) that extends 1 in. to 2 in. beyond the design area to add body without adding stiffness. You can use a water-soluble or cutaway interfacing, but tearaway stabilizer is not suitable for the stitch settings. You can also pin or hand-baste organza, batiste, or chiffon behind the design and then cut away the excess after beading. Once you have stabilized an area, it is helpful to use an embroidery hoop to frame the design while sewing.

I arranged pearl trim and raffia to give an ethnic flair to this plain bolero. Both trims are machine-couched to the garment. Because the design covers more than just the garment edges, I released the lining before doing any sewing.

TIP *To determine the largest-size embroidery hoop that you can use with your sewing machine, measure the size of the work area or the distance between the left edge of the presser foot and the body of the machine. Then select an embroidery hoop with that diameter, typically 7 in. to 8 in.*

Using a specialty presser foot such as the Pearls 'N Piping™ foot helps you guide the beads as you machine-couch them in place. Beading, piping, or bulky overlock feet have a groove at the bottom that is large enough to feed beads or piping up to 4mm in size. This groove guides the beads toward the needle as you negotiate straight lines and curves. An adjustable zipper foot is good for sewing beads along a finished edge and allows you to use beads that are larger than 4mm if you have a wider zigzag setting. The beads are guided along the edge of the foot. Be careful not to hit them with the needle; this can break the needle and the beads. Also, if your machine has a knee lever that lifts the presser foot, you'll be able to keep both hands on your work whenever you lift the foot to rotate the garment.

You can use either monofilament or all-purpose polyester thread in both the needle and bobbin. Otherwise, combine monofilament in the needle with all-purpose polyester or poly/cotton in the bobbin. Select whichever is the least visible with the trim you have chosen.

Practice is important for learning how to maneuver the trims under a bulky overlock foot or Pearls 'N Piping foot and to get the hang of what you can and cannot do. For example, sharp turns and inside corners aren't possible with larger beads (4mm) because the applied beads get in the way of the presser foot when you make the turn.

DESIGNER IDEA

Machine-couch rows of assorted beaded and sequin trims vertically and about 1 in. apart to embellish a simple skirt. If the skirt is lined, lift the lining away to avoid catching it when you sew the beads. If you use one to three of the same trims to outline the neckline of a sweater, you will have an outfit.

TIP *A sliding zipper foot allows you to turn tighter corners but requires more practice to use because there is no channel to guide the beads. Instead you must guide the beads along the side of the zipper foot. On the plus side, with a zipper foot you can place beads right on the edge of the garment, use slightly larger beads (the bead size must clear the zigzag stitch but doesn't have to fit under the channel in the presser foot), and you can couch rows of beads close together and turn square corners with large beads.*

MATERIALS

Beaded trim, molded beads, or cross-locked beads

Fabric marker

Presser foot, beading, piping, bulky overlock, or adjustable zipper

Thread, monofilament, all-purpose 100% polyester, or poly/cotton

Large crewel needle appropriate for the thickness of the thread

Stabilizer, optional

Embroidery hoop, 8 in. diameter, optional

Knee lever on the sewing machine, optional

MACHINE SETTINGS
FOR 2MM PEARLS OR BEADS

Thread tension: Regular
Stitch type: Zigzag
Stitch width: 2.5mm
Stitch length: 3.0mm

MACHINE SETTINGS
FOR 4MM PEARLS OR BEADS

Thread tension: Approximately 2½
Stitch type: Zigzag
Stitch width: 4.0mm or more
Stitch length: 3.0mm or more

1. Begin by deciding on a design. If you are not following a neckline or edge, mark the trim's placement line on the garment using a fabric marker.

2. Position the beaded trim under the beading or piping foot or to the right of the adjustable zipper foot, remembering to leave a tail at the beginning and the end of the trim. Set the zigzag width to the narrowest setting that will clear the beads, and set the stitch length to 0 or drop the feed dogs.

3. Holding the thread tails, sew three zigzag stitches.

4. Adjust the stitch width and length to the setting appropriate for your beads, then hold the fabric taut as you stitch over the beads. If you are not using an embroidery hoop, frame the work area with your hands.

5. Once the trim is sewn on, secure the threads by sewing three zigzag stitches at 0 per inch. Cut the threads, leaving 8-in. tails, and cut the excess trim, leaving the appropriate extension (molded bead trim has no string and can be cut next to the end stitch). Remove all of the extra beads from the tails, then thread all of the threads onto a crewel needle and pull them to the wrong side of the garment. Knot together.

TIP *You can easily dye pearl trim and individual prestrung pearls using Rit® or Tintex™ dye with interesting results. Just heat enough water to completely cover the trim and a small amount of dye in the microwave, then dunk the pearl trim or a section of strung pearls. Loose pearls are not manageable. Stir the trim to ensure an even color. As with all dyes, the intensity of the color increases the longer you let the trim steep in the dye, so rinse the trim once you've reached the desired shade. If you aren't happy with the color, you can dye the trim again.*

DESIGNER IDEA

You can enhance a ribbed cardigan by couching vertical rows of pearl trim following the ribbing of the cardigan. Using a combination of colors and sizes further enhances the surface interest.

Sequin trim
Fabric marker
Pearls 'N Piping foot
Thread, monofilament and polyester
*   or cotton/polyester*
Large crewel needle appropriate for
*   the thickness of the thread*
Stabilizer, optional
Embroidery hoop, optional
Knee lever on the sewing
*   machine, optional*

DESIGNER IDEA

To create a border effect, couch multiple rows of sequin trim along the lower edge of a skirt by combining straight rows with zigzag designs and shaped curves. Be sure to draw placement lines on the right side of the skirt first.

Couching sequin trim by machine

Sequin trim is appropriate to use along edges, hems, and within accessible areas of the garment's body. Because the trim is flexible and not bulky, you can cross it over itself and stitch over two layers.

Apply stabilizer if necessary, and if possible, place the portion of the garment you are embellishing in an embroidery hoop. If not, frame the area with your hands while couching. Use monofilament thread in the needle and polyester or cotton/polyester thread in the bobbin. Also, if your machine has a knee lever that lifts the presser foot, you'll be able to keep both hands on your work whenever you lift the foot to rotate the garment.

Machine-couched sequin trim meanders around the neckline of this T-shirt. To add extra flair, I removed individual sequins from the same trim and applied them using the beads with sequins stitch, the backstitch/flat stitch, and the sequin with loop stitch.

Thread tension: 2 to 3
Stitch type: Zigzag
Stitch width: 5.0mm or more
Stitch length: 3.0mm or more

**MACHINE SETTINGS FOR
STRAIGHT STITCHING SEQUIN TRIM**

Thread tension: 2 to 3
Stitch type: Straight
Needle position: Center
Stitch length: 4.0mm or more

1. Begin by deciding on a design. If not following a neckline or edge, mark the trim's placement line on the garment using a fabric marker.

2. Hold the trim so the sequins overlap from back to front (so you'll sew with the nap). Pull the sequins off the back end of the trim to create a tail about 4 in. long, which you'll fasten neatly after you've finished couching. Insert the sequins into the presser foot guide, then pull the tail through to extend behind the foot.

3. If your sewing machine has a knot stitch, be sure to use it at both the beginning and end of your sewing. If your sewing machine does not have a knot stitch, just pull your top

and bobbin threads to the underside of the fabric after sewing and knot them together by hand. Do not backstitch to secure your stitches.

4. Sew the sequin trim in place, following the placement line and letting the presser foot guide the trim. When finished, cut off the extra trim, leaving a 4-in. tail.

5. Remove the sequins on the tail from their supporting threads, then use a crewel needle to pass the threads to the wrong side of the garment and tie them together.

TIP *You can glue sequin trim to handbags, tote bags, belts, and even garments. To do so, use flexible fabric glue that is compatible with how you plan to clean the item. Some glues are both washable and dry-cleanable. For more control, select a glue that is not runny, and use a cotton swab or small brush to apply glue just to the chainstitch on the back side of the sequin trim.*

Machine-Sewing Loose Beads

You can easily sew on individual beads by machine if you first string them onto a holding thread. The best thing about the following technique is that you can combine a variety of beads, and you can use large beads because you are not limited by the width of the zigzag stitch on your machine. Practice this technique using the beads you'll work with on scrap fabric so you understand how much space to leave for each size bead.

You can use a decorative cord to hold the beads and invisible thread to couch them in place, or use invisible thread to hold the beads and a contrasting or invisible thread to couch the beads in place. The holding cord must be smooth enough to slide after it is couched to the fabric, fine enough to fit through the beads, and strong enough to hold them. Smooth, thin decorative cords, 100% polyester thread, and monofilament all work.

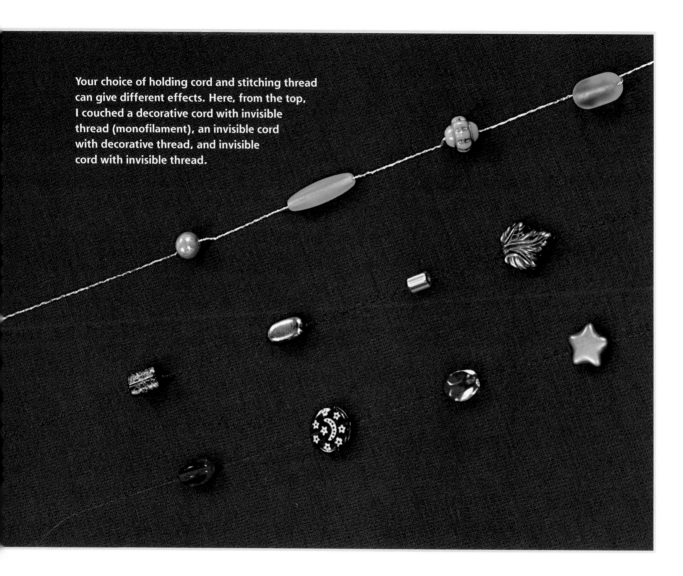

Your choice of holding cord and stitching thread can give different effects. Here, from the top, I couched a decorative cord with invisible thread (monofilament), an invisible cord with decorative thread, and invisible cord with invisible thread.

It is more manageable to work with the holding cord or thread on the spool than to cut it to a specific length. This allows you to sit the spool with the strung beads in a coffee mug or similar container to avoid tangles.

Before sewing, you can plan and mark the position of each bead, or just space them randomly without any marking, which I like to do. Unless you'll be aligning the holding cord with a garment edge, it's a good idea to mark a placement line for it. You can position the beads at regular intervals without marking if you make the same number of stitches between each when you couch over the cord.

DESIGNER IDEA

Once you get used to this technique of machine-sewing loose beads, you can try couching several different decorative threads plus the beads on a separate holding thread at one time, or try using decorative stitches instead of a zigzag stitch. There are many possible variations.

MATERIALS

Chalk or air-erasable marker

Beads, alike or assorted

Embroidery foot or pintuck foot

Holding thread, decorative or invisible

*Needle thread, decorative, 100% polyester,
    or monofilament*

*Bobbin thread, 100% polyester or
    bobbin/lingerie*

MACHINE SETTINGS

Thread tension: Regular

Stitch type: Zigzag

Stitch width: 2.0mm

Stitch length: 2.0mm

1. Using a chalk marker or an air-erasable marker, mark the placement line on the right side of the garment.

2. If you want to mark the bead positions, place a chalk mark across the stitch line where you want each to fall. The closest spacing possible between individual beads or groups of beads is a presser foot length (or about 1 in.) because the presser foot must clear the edge of the previous couched bead in order to be able to sew the next bead in place. (You can get around this limitation by not pulling the holding thread and bead close to the fabric until it clears the back of the presser foot.

A sewing machine makes quick work of beaded embellishment. Here I strung individual beads of assorted shapes and sizes onto a decorative silver holding cord, which I then sewed to the dress using a zigzag stitch.

3. String the beads onto the holding cord, then position the cord under the presser foot, leaving an 8-in. tail. Pull 8-in. tails of thread from the bobbin and needle and hold taut while you sew a few stitches over the holding cord, then secure the sewing threads and holding cord by wrapping them around a straight pin that is pinned to the fabric.

4. Next, guide the holding cord under the presser foot and zigzag over it. Stop with the needle down to the right of the cord and raise the presser foot. Swing

the holding cord to the left, out of the way of the foot and needle.

5. Lower the foot and, without catching the holding thread, sew for a sufficient distance to create a space for the bead to lie in once the cord is pulled tight and the next section sewn down. Stop with the needle down on its right swing to hold the fabric in place.

6. Raise the foot and slide one bead up the holding cord. Swing the bead behind the needle, forming a loop, and butt the holding cord next to the left side of the needle.

7. Lower the foot and continue to zigzag over the holding cord for the desired space between beads. To eliminate slack in the loop behind the presser foot, pull the holding cord from the front of the presser foot as you go. This will pull the bead against the fabric. (You won't be able to pull the bead completely against the fabric until the presser foot clears the bead position.)

8. Repeat steps 4 through 7 until as many beads as desired are attached.

9. Finish by bringing the sewing threads, holding threads, and any cords to the wrong side of the garment using a needle, then tying a knot.

DESIGNER IDEA

String colorful beads in assorted shapes and sizes onto a holding cord that stretches, then couch them to the neckline and sleeve hems of a T-shirt. Use stretch elastic or, better still, purchase stretch bead and jewelry cord, which is available at sources that sell beads as well as at some fabric and craft stores. One brand to look for is Stretch Magic Cord™, which comes in several colors and three thicknesses.

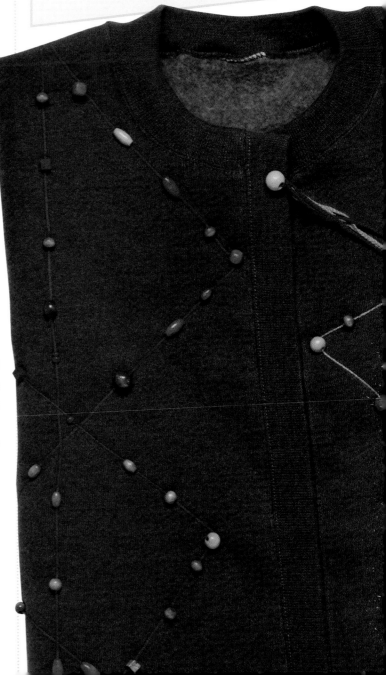

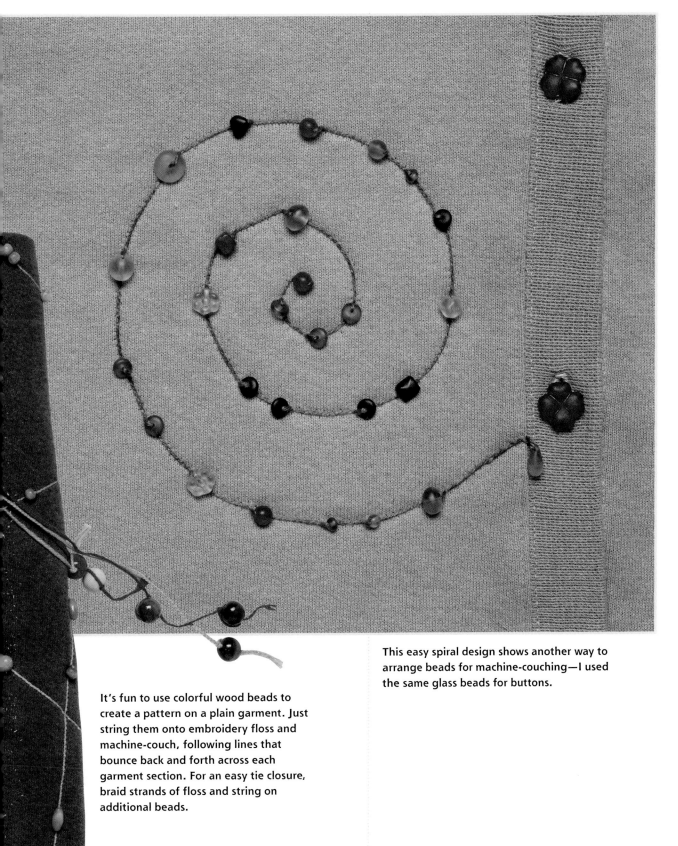

This easy spiral design shows another way to arrange beads for machine-couching—I used the same glass beads for buttons.

It's fun to use colorful wood beads to create a pattern on a plain garment. Just string them onto embroidery floss and machine-couch, following lines that bounce back and forth across each garment section. For an easy tie closure, braid strands of floss and string on additional beads.

Trims

Store-bought trims are wonderful sources for quick embellishment. Since most trims are ready to use with little or no preparation, these embellishments are easy to do. Look for interesting by-the-yard trims such as fringe, ribbon, braid, or lace, or choose fancy trims such as embroidered appliqués, feather trim, or silk flowers that complement your garment. Remember that the embellishment doesn't have to be noticeable from across the room to be successful. For example, just adding a change of texture to the edge of a neckline with velvet or grosgrain ribbon will enliven the entire garment. On the flip side, adding feather trim to the garment edge is fun and really gets everyone's attention.

Fringe

The typical place (and my favorite) to add fringed trim is at the edge of a garment where it will make the transition from the garment to the wearer's body or other layers of clothing more interesting. Depending upon the look desired, you can add a fringed trim or unravel the garment edge to create a self-fringe.

Fringed trims are typically held together at the top edge by a simple or decorative band called a header. If you make your own fringed trim (see pp. 21–27), you can attach it to a pretty ribbon or a plain length of twill tape. The header is normally sewn to the wrong side of the garment so it doesn't show, but if your fringe has a decorative header or if you've made it on a pretty ribbon, you can place the header on the outside of the garment. If you do this, you'll probably need to sew along both edges of the header.

When applying fringe all around a neckline or hemline, begin and end at a seam and plan to finish and overlap the header ends appropriately. For any fringe application, the manner in which you finish the header ends varies with the thickness of the header, so be sure to read "Finishing Fringe Header Ends" on p. 47 before beginning.

Attaching fringed trim

Unless you want to avoid the look of topstitching or are adding fringed trim to a hard-to-reach area of the garment, attach the trim by machine. Some fringes are unruly and tangle-prone; these are often sold with

Ball fringe gives a jaunty finish to just about anything—it's especially fun on denim. If you have trouble finding just the right color, you can dye the trim, as I did. The stylized flower was machine-embroidered using a combination of straight and decorative stitches, as well as free-motion stitching.

an additional row of chainstitching to secure the bottom end of the strands. This row of chainstitching is easy to remove, but for easy handling, leave it in place until after you sew on the fringe.

Beaded fringe trims must be handled a little differently from other types (see pp. 21–27 for an explanation of how to cut and sew them on).

MATERIALS

Fringe trim

Thread, all-purpose cotton, polyester, or poly/cotton to match the fabric

Standard foot; zipper foot when necessary

1. Fold under or stabilize the starting end of the fringe header using a zigzag stitch.

2. Position the trim either on top of the garment edge or under the edge, depending on how well you like the look of the header, then pin the fringe in place. Fold under or mark and stabilize the other end of the header.

3. Stitch the header in place with the right side of the garment facing up as you sew. If the ends of the fringe don't overlap, begin by sewing a knot stitch, sewing five stitches using a stitch length of 0, or backstitching a short distance. Use a zipper foot when the standard foot does not allow you to get close enough to the fringe.

4. Once the fringe is sewn on, lock in the stitches using a knot stitch or backstitch or by sewing five stitches in place using a stitch length of 0.

ENLIVENING GARMENTS WITH FRINGE

Since fringed trims are available in an assortment of styles, you can use fringe on lots of different garments without repeating or copying your other looks. Single-color, multicolor, short, long, soft, stiff, wispy, bulky, looped—even tassel and pom-pom—fringes come in various sizes and textures and are easy to machine-sew onto a finished garment.

What is fun about soft fringe is that the movement always attracts attention. Wispy, delicate fringe is best for delicate fabrics. Bold, thick, ropelike fringe looks wonderful on outerwear and bulky garment edges. When you want something dressy or glittery, use handmade or purchased beaded fringe (to make your own, see pp. 21–27). But the choice is really yours—select a type or style that is an obvious add-on or one that looks like an extension of the garment.

Here are some ways and places I like to use fringe:

- At hems on skirts, tops, sleeves, dresses, and pants

- To rim jacket and shirt collars

- At the neckline, front edge, and hem of a simple, boxy jacket or cardigan

- To outline yokes and pockets

- At the top edge of a tote bag or purse

- Along the flap, lower edge, or around the entire outer edge of a purse

- At both ends of a neck scarf or shawl or around the entire shawl

TIP *Topstitch the edge of the garment to hold the trim in place if the garment fabric is crisp and stable. If the edge of the garment already has topstitching or binding, use monofilament thread in the needle and all-purpose thread in the bobbin.*

You could also hand-sew the header to the wrong side of the garment using a running stitch.

Ready-made fringe adds a fast, swingy edge to a hemline. I chose glass-bead fringe here, but you could use rayon chainette or any number of other fringe types.

TIP *Ball fringe and tassel fringe look great along the neckline of a T-shirt or sweater but once they're sewn on, the neckline won't stretch, so choose a garment with a generous neck opening.*

Attaching beaded fringe trim

When adding beaded fringe trim, you'll need to secure the thread that connects the beads to the header before cutting the trim to the desired size. If you don't, the beads will fall off when you cut the header.

Put a zipper foot on your machine and sew using a straight stitch; this will allow you to get close to the beaded edge of the holding tape or header. (Of course,

DESIGNER IDEA

• *Create a new and curvy fringed hemline on a long skirt or tunic by adding store-bought fringe to an asymmetric wavy line that you draw on the right side of the garment. Try on the garment to make sure that you like the placement line, then attach the fringe using a machine topstitch and trim away the excess garment fabric near the fringe stitch line.*

• *Try using ball fringe or tassel fringe around the upper or lower edge of a purse or tote.*

FINISHING FRINGE HEADER ENDS

The way you finish the ends of a fringe header depends mostly on how bulky it is and on whether you are finishing each end separately or joining the ends (for instance, when sewing fringe all around a neckline). Before you begin your embellishment, take a look at the fringe header to see how it is woven, whether it is prone to raveling, and if it can be folded under.

For Separate Ends

If the header is not bulky, you can just fold under the ends and sew them to the garment when you sew on the fringe. If the header is too bulky to fold under, you should stabilize the ends using a zigzag stitch so they don't ravel. To do this, cut a piece of fringe trim a little longer than needed, then zigzag across the header about ½ in. from one end (the end at which you'll start sewing). Cut off the excess header just beyond the stitches,

then measure and mark the exact trim length needed and stabilize the other end.

For Joined Ends

If the header is not bulky, you can sew the ends together and press open the seam allowance, or you can simply fold under each end and abut them. If the header is too thick to sew in a regular seam, I sometimes slightly overlap the zigzagged ends or turn back one end and lap it over the other end. You can also trim each end right next to the zigzag and then butt the ends together.

TIP *If the header has a decorative pattern or the fringe itself is spaced out (like the ball fringe shown on the denim jacket in the photo on p. 44), be sure to sew the zigzag so that the pattern or spacing will begin where you wish when you put the trim on the garment.*

you can slipstitch the header to your garment by hand if you don't want to see a row of machine stitches.)

MATERIALS

Beaded fringe trim
Thread, all-purpose cotton, polyester, or poly/cotton thread to match the fabric
Zipper foot

1. Stabilize one end of the fringe header by sewing by hand or using a machine straight stitch about ½ in. from the cut edge. If the header is beginning to ravel or any beads are beginning to unfasten, place the stitching where the threads are holding and cut away the excess header, leaving a ½-in. seam

allowance. Then remove any remaining fringe from the seam allowance by pulling away the individual beads.

2. Position the fringe header either on top of the garment edge or under the edge, depending on how well you like the look of the header. Pin the fringe in place, turning under the stabilized starting end, then mark and stabilize the other end of the header. Cut off the excess, leaving a ½-in. seam allowance, and turn under the allowance. If you are doing a circular application, such as a hem, begin and end at a side seam or center back seam; plan to overlap the ends appropriately.

3. Using a zipper foot, stitch the header in place with the right side of the garment facing up as you sew. If the ends of the fringe don't overlap, begin by sewing a knot stitch (or sew five stitches using a stitch length of 0). As you reach the end, turn under the cut end of the header.

4. Once the fringe is sewn on, lock in the stitches using a knot stitch or backstitch or by sewing five stitches in place using a stitch length of 0. Cut the threads, leaving a 12-in. tail, then thread the tail onto a hand-sewing needle and slipstitch the folded end of the header in place.

Self-fringing a garment hem

Self-fringe is easy to do, requires little sewing, and always matches. If a garment has a hem allowance that is 1 in. or deeper, you can fringe both the outside and the hem allowance to create a double layer of fringe.

On ready-made garments, hems are the easiest part to self-fringe. Select simple garments, such as skirts, dresses, tunics, and unlined jackets, that are made of fabrics that unravel easily. Good choices are

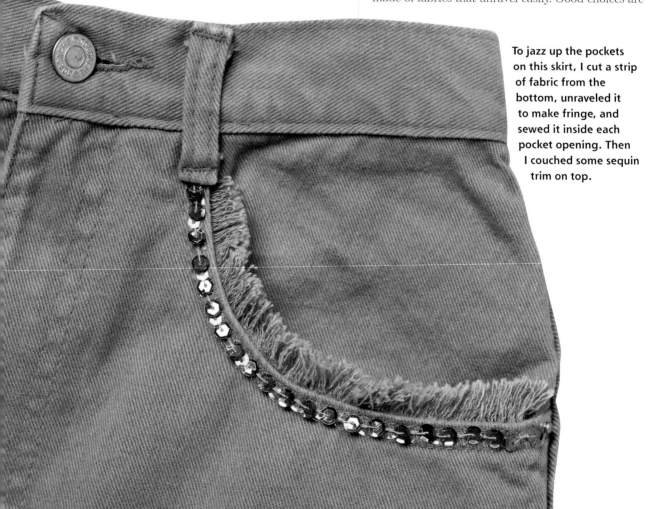

To jazz up the pockets on this skirt, I cut a strip of fabric from the bottom, unraveled it to make fringe, and sewed it inside each pocket opening. Then I couched some sequin trim on top.

There are many creative ways in which you can use fringe to achieve different looks.

After self-fringing a garment, try placing a store-bought fringe behind the self-fringe and zigzagging in place.

Create a soft, upright fringe along the top of a pair of jeans. To do this, cut away or remove the topstitching along the waist edge, then sew a zigzag stitch where you would want the fringe to begin (about ¾ in. to 1 in. down). Make sure you also cut the top of the waistband along the fold. Next, simply unravel the fibers to fringe the edge. If you want to fringe the entire width of the waistband, it is not necessary to add the zigzag stitching because the topstitching that is already along the waist edge of the waistband serves the same purpose.

Another way to fringe the waistband on a pair of jeans or a jeans skirt is by adding one or more decorative ribbons and braids along the waist seam, then fringing the waistband above the trim.

Self-fringing the edge of a garment gets more adventurous when you start fringing shaped edges on a jacket (not an Armani® jacket, please).

Place a zigzag about 1 in. from the finished edge that you wish to fringe, cut off just enough of the garment edge to remove the stitching (about ⅛ in.), and fringe away. Good places to fringe are the neckline and front edge, the collar edge, and lapels. Remember that fringing a few selective areas has more impact than fringing everything in sight.

Fine-gauge single knits and synthetic fleece can also be fringed easily—just cut into the fabric at frequent intervals.

Take self-fringe a step further by fringing strips of fabric to embellish areas of your chosen garment. Buy a small amount of a colorful or patterned fabric, such as a plaid, check, or stripe, just to make fringe for embellishment. Another source for fringe material could be from an alteration. If you shorten a skirt, why not fringe the excess fabric and embellish a sweater?

If you'd like to fringe a summer skirt, cut or tear 1-in. strips of lightweight fabric and fringe about ¼ in. along both long edges. Position the strips vertically, and stitch in place using a straight or decorative stitch.

coarse cotton, raw silk, linen, woolens, challis, and denim; loose weaves are easiest of all. There are some neat possibilities when you fringe patterned fabrics, such as prints, plaids, checks, and stripes, and fabrics having different-colored warp and woof fibers.

1. Start by stabilizing the top of the hem using a medium zigzag stitch (2mm to 2.5mm wide and long), being sure to sew through both layers. If the hem is deeper than the desired fringe depth, just stabilize where you would like to start the fringe.

2. Cut the hemline along the foldline. This separates the hem layer at the lower edge only.

3. Unravel the crosswise threads on both the outside and inside hem layers, stopping at the zigzag stitch.

TIP *If you'd like the fringe to be deeper than the hem allowance, take out the stitches securing the hem, then either cut off the hem allowance or unfold it and press out the crease. Stabilize wherever you'd like the fringe to begin. This will result in only one layer of fringe.*

Tassels

Tassels can punctuate, draw attention to, or add a finishing touch to corners, points, or sashes on garments and home furnishings. Think tie belts, points on collars, corners on yokes, and side slits on tunics, dresses, and sweaters. Tassels are great additions on zipper pulls on jackets and other outerwear garments, on sweaters, and on handbags.

Store-bought tassels are available for use on both clothing and home furnishings and can be used interchangeably. Although some decorator tassels are too large or bulky for garment use, many more are just perfect.

TIP *If you are embellishing a washable garment, it is important to learn if a tassel is washable before you buy it.*

Attaching tassels

To attach a tassel, position it so that most of the hanging loop is hidden behind the garment edge,

then sew in place by hand using a slipstitch. Hide the thread knot between the tassel and garment.

When adding a tassel where you would see the inside of the garment and therefore see the hanging loop, either cover the loop with another trim or insert the loop between the garment and the facing. To do the latter:

1. Remove just enough stitches along the edge to insert the hanging loop.

2. Insert the loop between the layers and sew in place.

3. Restitch the edge using a slipstitch.

Adding tassels to the ends of a tie belt or sash

For the ends of tie belts and sashes, I like to use the types of tassels that can be purchased from drapery departments. You can either buy individual tassels or sets of two that are connected by a rope. The latter are typically used as tiebacks for drapery.

1. If the tassel's top cord is thick, cut the cord 1 in. above the tassel and untwist the cords so that the strands lie next to one another. Then machine-sew across all the strands to hold them together and flat.

2. Cut off ⅛ in. to ¼ in. from both ends of the belt. This way you will be able to pull away both the stitches and the seam allowance.

3. Press under a new ¼-in. seam allowance (see the illustration on the facing page).

4. Machine-baste along the center of the belt for about 2 in.

5. Next, machine-baste parallel to the end a distance equal to one-half the width of the belt.

6. Turn in and press the corners diagonally using the basting lines as a guide.

7. Insert the tassel between the layers and edgestitch the ends.

Using fringed trim to make tassels

Although there are many wonderful ready-made tassels, they don't always match or flatter your garment and they can be expensive. You can easily roll fringed trim around itself to form beautiful tassels to decorate garments and accessories.

Adding even the simplest store-bought tassels to the ends of a plain tie belt not only adds interest but also improves the drape when you tie the belt. Tassels come in myriad styles; I always enjoy choosing the perfect kind.

Step 2

R/S

Cut

Step 3

R/S

Press back a ¼-in. seam allowance.

Step 5

R/S

Machine-baste along the center.

Machine-baste a perpendicular line the same distance away from the folded edge.

Step 6

R/S

Press in the corners diagonally.

MATERIALS

⅛ yd. (or less) of fringe per tassel

Fabric glue

Cotton swab or small brush

Braided trim, fine cords, or tiny beads

MAKING A TASSEL USING FRINGED TRIM

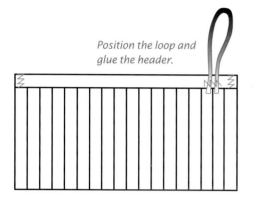

Position the loop and glue the header.

Zigzag stitches

Glue

Roll the fringe and glue the end.

1. Stabilize one end of the fringe header by sewing a medium to wide machine zigzag stitch about ½ in. away from the cut edge, then cut off the excess next to the zigzag stitching. To get an idea of how much fringe to use, tightly roll the top of the fringe until you like the size, then mark, stabilize, and cut the other end.

2. To make a hanging loop for attaching the tassel, unfasten a few strands from the fringe material. Cut the strands to a length of 3½ in. to 4 in. and fold in half to form a loop. Attach both ends of the loop to one end of the fringe header using a straight stitch or a zigzag stitch (see the top illustration at left).

3. Using a cotton swab or a small brush, apply glue to the fringe header and roll up the strip of fringe, starting at the loop end (see the bottom illustration at left).

4. Once the glue has dried, fasten the outer end of the fringe using several hand stitches that go through all of the layers at the top of the tassel.

5. Embellish the top of the tassel by wrapping it with braided trim or fine cords or by covering it with tiny beads.

Lace

Most of the time you can sew lace embellishments successfully, beautifully, and better by machine than by hand, but each project is different.

Machine-sewing lace trim

Lace trims are perfect for overlays and insertions on a finished garment. It is usually easier to work with narrow lace formations than with clipped lace because the edges are firm and regular.

Use a thread that blends well with the type of lace. For example, you can use rayon machine-embroidery thread to sew rayon lace. Fine size A silk is strong and lustrous. Metallic embroidery thread, cotton embroidery thread, all-purpose cotton, 100% polyester, and cotton-covered polyester are other possibilities.

TIP *With the exception of appliqués, cut each length of lace longer than needed so you can you turn back and finish the ends.*

If you want to use a lace overlay, attach it along one edge only; leave the opposite edge loose. Overlays look good when placed horizontally above the hems of skirts, dresses, and tunics and on or near shoulder seams to create a yoke effect. They also look nice when placed vertically next to the front placket on shirts, blouses, and cardigan sweaters. For vertical overlays, stitch them in place along the edge that is next to the placket.

Lace insertions are stitched in place along both edges. You may either leave the garment fabric behind the lace or cut it away to create openwork bands on the garment, as shown in the photo at left. Insertions are synonymous with French hand-sewing, delicate vintage fashions, and romantic blouses and skirts, but you can use them to reflect your own fashion sensibility. For more modern applications, use insertions on simple dresses, placing several horizontal rows of lace above the hemline or above the armhole to create bands of lace in the yoke area. Using several rows of lace vertically on the front of a dress is also effective. Position the lace trim within the garment and stitch it in place along both edges.

Bias-cut garments such as this camisole are the perfect canvas on which to insert flattering diagonal bands of lace. The insertions follow the straight grain of the garment so it is easy to sew them in place.

Insertions and overlays look beautiful and interesting when stitched following the straight grain on simple bias-cut dresses, skirts, and tops. This creates diagonal bands of lace that are flattering to wear.

To sew on lace by machine:

1. Pin the lace trim in place.

2. Machine-sew the lace along one or both edges using a straight stitch or narrow zigzag stitch. You can stop at this step if you are using the lace as an overlay on the garment or if you are not going to cut away the fabric behind an insertion.

3. If desired, trim away the garment fabric from behind the lace, leaving a ¼-in. seam allowance. To cut away only the garment fabric, use your fingers to pinch the garment fabric between the rows of stitches and clip it carefully.

4. Press the seam allowance away from the lace trim.

5. Using a medium zigzag stitch, stitch the lace edge again from the right side.

DYEING LACE

Since the selection of lace in fashion colors is somewhat limited, consider buying white or ecru lace and then dying it yourself using a multifiber dye such as Rit or Tintex. These dyes work on a variety of fibers and are the easiest to use. First test a small piece of lace following the dye's package directions, and remember the lace doesn't have to match the fabric exactly.

Keep in mind that if you are not thrilled with the color, you can modify the color by dying the lace again. To tone down a primary color, use a neutral-color dye such as gray, ecru, or very small amounts of black or brown.

Change a pullover sweatshirt into a cardigan by cutting off the bottom ribbing and cutting open the front. Then either turn under the front edges or sew the removed ribbing to them. Here I added lace appliqués to the neckline and scalloped lace trim to the lower edge, which I embellished with small, purchased tassels and crystal beads.

Sewing clipped lace

Clipped lace offers many interesting possibilities for embellishing ready-to-wear because when you clip it following the various motifs, the resulting medallions don't have that cookie-cutter regularity that you get when you buy lace appliqués. A clipped lace border has a wonderful wavy effect along the edge. The contoured edge makes a nice transition from fabric to lace, but most importantly, it is more able to follow curved edges on the garment. Where necessary, you can clip into the border fol-

I dyed some white alençon lace a brassy green, clipped it, and sewed it to this classic merino cardigan. The appliqués look airy and open because I cut away the knit fabric behind each.

lowing a motif to help it conform to curves along the edge of the garment.

To decide how to use clipped lace, cut some motifs from your lace fabric, leaving a generous portion of net background around each. Also leave the net filling inside complicated areas and only cut around the basic shape. Then take time to play, pinning the shapes to your garment. This is my favorite part of the process because there are so many ways to position the lace. Keep in mind that grain is not an issue and the best placement is the one you like best.

You can sew on clipped lace by machine, as explained on p. 58. Whenever possible, sew the lace in place using all-purpose thread. If a second row of stitching is necessary, select the thread using the

LACE, LACE, LACE—WHAT'S AVAILABLE

Lace fabrics and trims are a wonderful source for embellishments. Don't limit lace to special-occasion garments, fragile fabrics, and romantic styles. Lace can be modern, traditional, romantic, funky, and even whimsical and is available in many forms to suit a variety of applications.

Knowing the types of lace that are available enables you to choose the one that works best for your design ideas.

Types of Lace

Alençon lace is also called reembroidered lace because each motif is outlined in a heavy cord. It typically has a floral motif on a fine net background.

Chantilly lace is lighter in weight than alençon and has a fine, threadlike cord outlining the motifs. The motifs are typically floral on a net background.

Venise lace, also called guipure lace, does not have a net background. This lace has a rich, three-dimensional surface and an open effect. The motifs range from floral to modern geometric designs.

Cluny is a heavier and less formal lace made of fairly heavy threads.

Lace Formations

Lace is made in a number of widths and forms suited for a variety of applications. Being aware of the available formations helps you make better use of lace fabrics and trims.

Wide lace is lace fabric that measures 36 in. or wider. In addition to being used to sew entire garments, it can be cut apart—or "clipped"—to make beautiful lace appliqués.

A **lace edge** is a trim with one scalloped edge and one straight edge. Narrow edges are used to trim necklines, sleeves, and hems. Wider edges, which can measure 10 in. to 18 in. wide, can be used as bold borders or for smaller garment sections such as sleeves, collars, and yokes.

Insertion is a trim that has two straight edges and is used flat. The garment fabric behind the insertion is normally clipped away.

Galloon has two scalloped edges and can be a narrow trim or wide lace.

Beading refers to any lace that has a row of holes through which a ribbon or trim can be woven. Beading is available as an edge, insertion, or galloon.

Lace appliqués are individual lace shapes that can be sewn to any part of a garment. They are also called medallions or motifs.

Clipping Lace

When standard lace formations don't do the trick, clipping allover laces opens up all sorts of wonderful possibilities. Most laces can be clipped apart into sections in a number of ways. Clip to create borders, panels, and individual motifs that form beautiful and interesting shapes that you can easily apply to garments and accessories.

Clipped lace may be machine-stitched, hand-stitched, or glued in place. Gluing is most suitable for accessories such as belts, hats, and handbags, whereas machine- or hand-sewing is most suitable for garments. If you plan to glue or hand-sew the lace to the item you are embellishing, cut the lace following the motif outline. If you plan to machine-sew the lace, cut the lace roughly around the motif or border because it will be easier to sew in place. You can then trim away the excess after you sew the lace.

Types of lace include (clockwise from upper left) allover lace, alençon lace, insertion, edge, galloon, beading, Chantilly lace, Venise appliqué, and Venise allover lace.

same parameters as for sewing lace trim. If you want a softer effect, sew clipped lace on by hand.

1. Pin the lace in place.

2. Using a straight stitch or a narrow zigzag, sew on the lace following the motif.

3. To remove excess netting, carefully cut along the stitched edge of each motif using appliqué scissors.

4. If the lace is fragile or very open and the garment fabric frays easily, stitch again using a narrow zigzag stitch, changing to a silk or embroidery thread that blends with the lace and if possible the fabric, too.

5. If you wish, trim away the garment fabric behind the lace to create a sheer pattern. To cut only the garment fabric, pinch it behind the lace motif center with your fingers and carefully clip, staying about ¼ in. away from the stitching.

Hand-sewing lace

The few reasons to hand-sew are to have possibly better control when the lace is placed over a shaped section of a garment, to sew invisibly, and because you enjoy hand-sewing. If you are using clipped lace, cut the motifs exactly as you want them to appear; don't leave extra net along the perimeter. Use a size 9 sharp or crewel needle and a single strand of all-purpose cotton, polyester, or poly/cotton thread.

1. Pin the lace trim or lace motif in place on the garment. When placing lace over a shaped area, try to pin with the garment on a dress form or the body. Otherwise be sure to try on the garment before sewing on the lace so you can be sure the contours lie smoothly.

2. Gently slipstitch the edge of the lace to the garment.

Instant ruffles

Vintage and imported place mats, tablecloths, and even bedspreads often have a wealth of cutwork or heavy lace details that you can cut apart and add to ready-made garments and accessories. I especially like to reuse the round or oval decorative borders that sometimes frame runners and small table toppers. When you attach the inside edge of these curved borders to a straight edge, such as the hem on a skirt, you get a pretty fluted ruffle. A border that is scal-

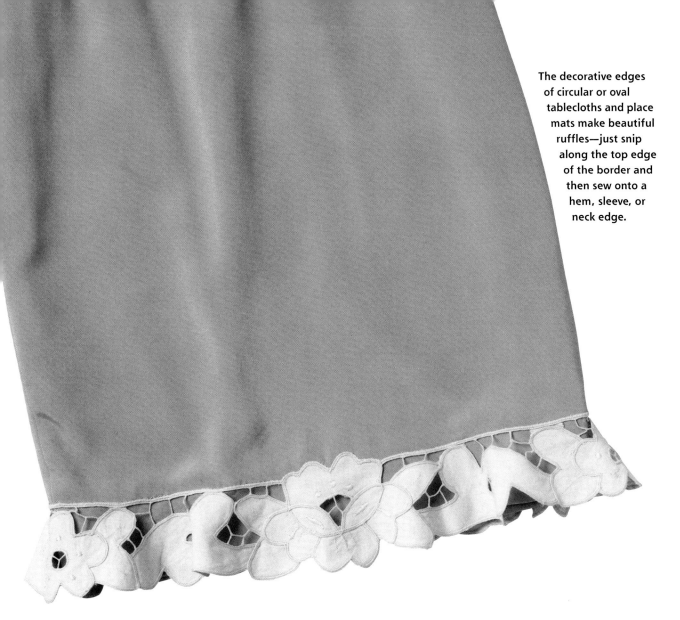

The decorative edges of circular or oval tablecloths and place mats make beautiful ruffles—just snip along the top edge of the border and then sew onto a hem, sleeve, or neck edge.

loped on the inside also works very well—your ruffle will have interesting flutes.

The easiest way to do create these ruffles is to find a border with an inside circumference equal to the circumference of the lower edge of the skirt. But the chances of that happening are slim, so you can use just a section of a larger border or combine two identical borders, cutting each from inner to outer edge on the straight grain and then sewing the cut edges together.

If you cut the border from a tablecloth, you'll need to include a seam allowance at the top for sewing it to your garment. Because of the curved edge, you'll probably need to use a little trial and error to figure how deep to cut the border so it will be long enough to go around your garment and at the same time make any motifs or patterns on the border meet pleasingly. Take the time to figure it out—you might need to cut the border in several pieces to keep the pattern symmetrical.

TIP *If the border has a line of satin stitching or other tight embroidery along its top edge, you won't need to add a seam allowance. Simply cut the border just above the stitches.*

MATERIALS

Tablecloth or other linen with a round or oval border
Needle thread, all-purpose or embroidery
Bobbin thread, all-purpose or bobbin/lingerie

1. Measure the edge of the garment you want to add the ruffle to, and cut enough curved sections from the tablecloth border to make a ruffle of that length when joined together. If the border does not have a satin stitch along the top edge, be sure to include enough solid fabric at the top edge (above the lace) to create a seam allowance.

2. If necessary, sew the sections together to form a ring. The way you do this will depend upon the kind of lace you're using, but a small zigzag stitch will probably be best.

3. Slip the ruffle over the garment, placing the wrong side of the ruffle against the right side of the garment with the top edge of the ruffle toward the top of the garment. Pin the ruffle around the lower edge, and baste it in place if necessary.

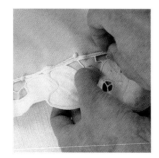

4. From the right side, sew the ruffle to the garment. If the ruffle has an embroidered top edge, stitch over it using a long zigzag stitch.

Ribbons and Braids

Ribbons and braids are easy to work with and come in a great selection of sizes, colors, and textures, making them perfect materials for creating embellishments. If you want to keep the stitches inconspicuous, use a straight stitch or a narrow zigzag. Or you can add another dimension by using a decorative stitch.

Some braids are flexible and follow curves nicely while staying flat against the garment. Ribbons and braids that are not flexible should be applied in straight lines or folded to follow corners.

Flat designs for flat trims

Create beautiful surface designs on the body of a simple jacket, skirt, or sweatshirt using sheer, velvet, or decorative ribbons. As you sew, you can fold miters into the ribbon whenever you want to turn a corner, so don't hesitate to come up with a design that has lots of zigs and zags.

MATERIALS

Fabric marker such as an air-erasable marker or white pencil
Decorative ribbons, ¼ in. to 1 in. wide
Thread, all-purpose or machine embroidery

1. Using a fabric marker, mark a line on the right side of the garment where you want one edge of the ribbon to be placed. Don't cut the ribbon to size until you have sewn the first side in place on the garment.

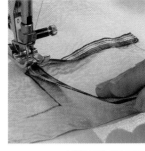

2. Turn under and press the end of the ribbon trim, then position the ribbon on top of the garment, lining up one edge with the marked line. Sew across the folded end of the ribbon

toward the marked line, being sure to sew a few stitches in place to secure the thread.

3. When you reach the corner, raise the presser foot and rotate the work. Lower the presser foot and sew close to the edge of the ribbon. If your design line turns corners, stop when you reach the first corner, make sure the needle is in the fabric, lift the presser foot, and turn the corner and manipulate the ribbon in one of the following ways.

To turn an outside corner, rotate the work, shift the edge of the ribbon to align with the marked line, lower the presser foot, and continue sewing.

To turn an inside corner, rotate the garment, then use a long pin to help you fold the ribbon diagonally, forming a miter that allows the side of the ribbon you are sewing to again follow the marked line.

You can also turn a corner by folding the ribbon back on itself— but only if both sides of the ribbon are attractive. To do so, just fold the ribbon back on

itself at whatever angle you like, rotate the garment, and make a stitch onto the adjacent edge of the ribbon. Rotate more if necessary and continue to sew along the edge.

4. Sew until just before you reach the end of the marked line, then cut away the excess ribbon, leaving a little extra so you can finish the end. Turn under the excess ribbon and sew to the end.

5. Rotate the work and continue sewing across the end and, rotating as necessary, along the remaining side. To finish, sew again across the first end.

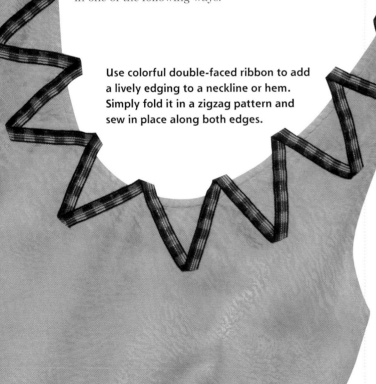

Use colorful double-faced ribbon to add a lively edging to a neckline or hem. Simply fold it in a zigzag pattern and sew in place along both edges.

Ribbons offer a host of design possibilities.

Try positioning parallel rows of ribbon in the lengthwise and crosswise directions on a garment to sew a decorative windowpane effect or positioning the rows on the bias to sew an attractive crosshatched or diamond design.

Use different colors of sheer ribbons on the same garment, attaching them so they cross in an interesting play of color. Jacquard ribbons are also interesting to use this way because you can mix patterns. Keep the ribbons a minimum of 2 in. apart or as much as 8 in., depending on the size and scale of the garment. Large, dramatic garments look best with wide spacing.

If you like a more random design, as I often do, attach ribbon following a diagonal step design starting at the upper left-hand corner as you face the garment, and sew the ribbon so it goes down, across, down, across, and so on until you reach the lower-right hem. If you get to the side seam before you get to the hem, continue the repeat until you reach the hem. To keep the effect slenderizing, make the vertical portions of the step pattern longer than the horizontal portions. After completing one row, sew additional rows to the left and right of the first row. Try to start and end at a seam or at the hemline. The effect is more interesting if each row is slightly different from the last, so you don't have to measure every change in the direction of the ribbon.

Use the previous technique to reshape the hem on a simple jacket or skirt. First mark the placement, then attach the upper edge of the ribbon. Cut the garment along the lower edge of the ribbon, and finish the garment edge using a zigzag stitch. Stitch the remaining edge of the ribbon to the finished edge. You could also do this in reverse along a neckline.

Add a wide ribbon trim around the lower edge of a skirt using a straight stitch along the ribbon edge, then center a machine-embroidery stitch over the other edge of the ribbon and sew it in place. If the garment fabric is lightweight, fuse a narrow strip of interfacing behind the area that will be machine-embroidered.

Try cutting each sleeve on a T-shirt vertically from the shoulder to the hem and finish the edges using a serger or a zigzag stitch. Topstitch ribbon onto the sleeve along each edge, turning under the ribbon at each end. Then add buttons or small beads every 2 in. to hold the trim together, overlapping the trim edges just enough to secure them as you sew. This technique is more dramatic on long sleeves but also looks attractive on three-quarter-length and short sleeves.

Brocade and jacquard ribbons make wonderful borders along the hems of skirts, dresses, and pants. Another way to use them is along the opening of a cardigan. If the cardigan has a button and buttonhole closure, you must remove the buttons to sew the trim, then sew the buttons back on. On the buttonhole side, leave the side of the trim that is nearest the edge unstitched so that you can still button the cardigan. The buttons will be covered by the trim when you button up the front.

Before attaching ribbon or seam binding to a garment, run a colorful stitch along one edge of the trim to create a dimensional edge. Use the rolled hem on a serger or try using some machine-embroidery stitches.

Another way to add a trim is to cut 1-in.-wide bias strips of sheer or lightweight fabric and don't finish the edges. Gather the center of the bias strip and sew it onto the neckline and sleeves of a top, T-shirt, or around the bottom edge of a skirt. As you wash the garment, the top edges of the trim will fray a little and look soft and feathery.

Swirls and raised-edge designs for flat trims

When you sew on one edge of a ribbon (or any other stable trim) along a curved line or in a spiral, the loose edge will lift away from the garment, creating a three-dimensional ruffled effect. This can look terrific on various areas of a garment. Rayon seam binding is nice to use this way because it has a soft hand that doesn't overpower most garments, even when you use a lot of it.

You can sew simple loops and turns over large areas of a garment or confine the embellishment to accessible edges. Keep the design light and airy by having lots of space between the loops, or densely cover the garment with spirals or concentric circles.

For the dense look, start by shaping the end of the ribbon into a small loop near the center of the design space. Using a simple straight stitch, sew the loop and continue sewing in circles, going around the last circle stitched until you fill out the area. Don't try to sew a perfect circle; in fact the shape could be oval or paisley, and variations in the spacing and shape make the raised effect interesting. Then you could continue sewing to the center of the next area and repeat the process.

> **TIP** *If you would like to sew allover ribbon swirls on a sweatshirt, consider cutting the sweatshirt open along the side seams (including all or most of the sleeves). You may be able to leave the sleeve cuffs intact. After you finish sewing the ribbon, you can restitch the side seams. This technique is easiest to do on flat and accessible areas of the garment.*

To create a quirky ruffled trim, mark a curved pattern on your garment, then sew rayon seam binding over it, stitching along one edge of the binding only. The unstitched edge will lift and flute.

TIP *Rayon seam binding comes in an array of wonderful colors, is inexpensive, and best of all is lightweight and soft. Preshrink the trim before using by soaking it in hot water, squeezing then blotting the excess water, and pressing with a dry iron to dry it.*

MATERIALS

Fabric marker

Presser foot, standard or ribbon

Seam binding or lightweight ribbon, about ½ in. wide

Thread, all-purpose or machine embroidery

1. Mark the placement for the trim using a fabric marker on the right side of the garment. There is no need to mark every placement line if you plan to sew concentric circles that will heavily cover an area of the garment. Instead, mark the starting point and the outer edge of the shape you plan to sew.

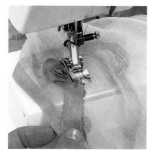

2. Using either a standard or ribbon presser foot, start sewing the trim at the center of a loop or motif and continue along the marked line or to fill the area.

3. Stop sewing a short distance from the end, and cut the ribbon a little longer than you need so that you can turn under and stitch across the end.

DESIGNER IDEA

Densely cover the collar of a jacket or sweater using velvet ribbon swirls.

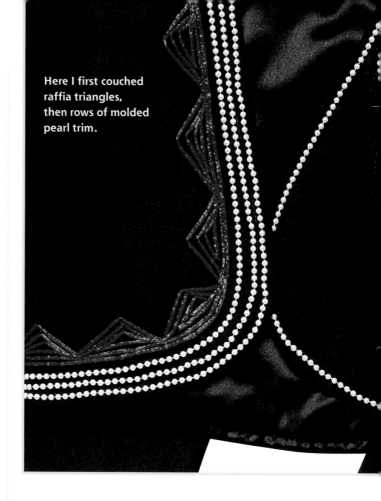

Here I first couched raffia triangles, then rows of molded pearl trim.

Round trims and cords

I especially like to use round trims on simple jackets, cardigan sweaters, and boleros. Be sure to select soft trims that are flexible and won't overpower the weight of the garment. The colors can be matching and subtle or patterned and wild. Arrange the trim to follow the garment edge, in straight lines or to echo a pattern in the garment fabric, or create decorative patterns that squiggle off the edge.

You can embellish any areas that are easy to reach with a machine, such as necklines, hems, and other edges. When you plan the design, try to start and end at an inconspicuous place, such as at a shoulder or side seam, so you can secure the ends of the trim unobtrusively. Leave tails of trim at each end so you can finish them after they are sewn to the garment.

Any of the machine feet intended to ride over piping and work with a zigzag or on your serger will make it easy to guide the round trim (these include the Pearls 'N Piping foot, bulky overlock foot, braiding foot, and narrow rolled hem foot). If your machine has a knee pedal to lift the presser foot, that will also help. Stabilize the design if you're working on a single layer of fabric rather than along the edges of the garment (see p. 75), then hoop the area of the garment to be embellished or frame it with your hands while sewing.

Yarns and narrow cords are easy to couch in place. You can keep the stitch invisible either by using monofilament thread in the needle or by matching the needle thread to the trim. Experiment on a scrap to find the best stitch setting. If the stitch length is too long for the trim, the trim will squiggle left and right with each swing of the needle, which can be an interesting look. Shortening the stitch length will help the trim follow a placement line. (To sew on larger cords and tubular trims without flattening them, see the sidebar at right.)

MATERIALS

Stabilizer, optional
Disappearing fabric marker or chalk
Embroidery hoop, optional
Presser foot, Pearls 'N Piping, bulky overlock, braiding, or narrow rolled hem
Soft and pliable cords, tubing, spaghetti straps, knitting yarns
Needle thread, monofilament or all-purpose
Bobbin thread, all-purpose
Tapestry needle

MACHINE SETTINGS

Needle tension: Reduce the tension one to three increments
Stitch type: Zigzag or blindstitch
Stitch setting to couch over narrow cords and yarns: Experiment to find the right setting

KEEPING ROUND TRIM ROUND

Some dimensional trims and cords look best if you avoid flattening them when you sew them on. You can sew them to the garment invisibly by using a machine zigzag or blindstitch. To do this, work along the edge of the trim using the narrowest possible stitch setting that doesn't skip areas or slip off the trim; start with a 2mm-wide and 4mm-long zigzag or blindstitch. Once sewn

on this way, the trim will roll over the stitches and keep its three-dimensional effect.

If your trim is bulky, incorporate an attractive way to finish the cut ends into the design. One option is to curve and tuck the ends under the rest of the trim just before stitching. You may have to sew the ends into place by hand.

1. To find the best placement for the trim, place the garment on a dress form, on a body, or on a hanger. Using a disappearing fabric marker or chalk, mark the placement line on the outside of the garment.

2. Place the garment under the presser foot. Thread the trim through the groove in the foot, pulling a 4-in. tail behind the needle. To begin, use a knot stitch to lock in the stitch, then adjust the machine to the zigzag setting and sew over the trim as you guide it along the placement line. When you are done, lock

in the stitch using a knot stitch and cut off the excess trim and threads, leaving 4-in. tails.

3. To finish the trim ends, either thread them through a tapestry needle and pass them to the wrong side along with the top sewing thread, or wrap them to the wrong side and secure them with a few hand stitches.

Fancy Trims

Thoughtful placement of fancy trims makes it easy to convert bland garments into boutique-worthy creations. Store-bought embroidered appliqués, silk flowers and leaves, and feather trims are easy to attach by hand or machine with dramatic results. Removable feather edging is versatile and practical, letting you dress up necklines and hemlines when you so desire and allowing you to embellish a variety of garments by reusing the same trim.

Embroidered trims

Check your trimmings store for wonderful embroidered appliqués—you can find them in many sizes, singly or joined together.

Embroidered appliqués in all manner of motifs are readily available at trimming stores. Use them to embellish collars, pockets, cuffs, or whatever. I placed these floral appliqués so they overlap this workshirt's collar edge to soften the shape.

Create an easy and effective 3-D appliqué by using silk flowers. Attach them with rhinestones, nail heads, or tiny buttons.

Floral motifs are common, but you can also find juvenile shapes such as ducks or themed pieces such as badges, which you can then sew to a collar or pocket flap or scatter over a garment. You can use the joined motifs as you would ribbon, but you'll be able to curve them along necklines or bend them around corners. Just pin them in place and sew them on by hand or machine, using whichever method seems best for the motif at hand.

Silk flowers

Bridal and millinery departments are a great source of small fabric flowers and leaves that you can use to add a three-dimensional flourish to a garment. Arrange them, corsagelike, on a lapel, or scatter them in a controlled or random pattern that suits your garment. Not all cloth flowers are washable, so test before attaching to a garment you plan to launder.

To maintain the dimension of the flowers, attach them in one or two spots; don't try to secure them along all edges. Let the shape of each flower or leaf dictate the best location for securing—in the center, or near one end, or at two petals, for instance. Of course, you can sew fabric flowers to your garment by hand, but why not attach them with a flourish? I like to fasten them with a small bead, button, or rhinestone.

TIP *Rhinestones come with sew-on bases or push-on prong settings. Both are easy to use but the prong settings are too short to secure on thick fabrics.*

Feather boa edging

What could be more glamorous (or more fun) than a wreath of soft feathers framing your face or wrist? Feather boas made from marabou, ostrich, or cock feathers are available in natural colors as well as in fanciful dyed colors and multicolor combinations—

If you yearn for flirty feather-trimmed clothes, try a button-on boa collar. All you have to do is sew strategically placed buttons to the garment and corresponding elastic loops to the boa.

and also with a mix of feather types. Boas typically come in 2-yd. lengths, but you can cut them to use along necklines and edges or to make perfect little poofs to trim pockets, handbags, or hats.

You can sew a boa directly to a garment or, better still, make it removable. Removable feather trim makes the garment versatile, since you can wear the feathers when you are "in the mood" and remove them when exotic isn't the thing. Also, since feathers don't do well in the wash, you can clean the garment without having to clean the feathers—making virtually any garment from a T-shirt to a gown a good canvas for a feather frill.

TIP *Attaching feather trim directly to the garment edge is fast and easy. First, secure the ends of the trim as explained in step 1 on the facing page, then pin it in place along the edge. Sew it on by hand using a whipstitch and thread that matches the garment.*

The easiest way to create a removable boa edging is by using elastic loops and small buttons. These loops are lightweight and easy to use—they come attached to corded trim, which is sold by the yard at sewing and trim stores. They're the perfect size to pair with flat, ½-in.-diameter buttons. To make a button-on boa, simply sew buttons strategically to the edge you want to embellish and sew corresponding elastic loops to the boa. Boas have multiple cords at the center that you can feel but won't see unless you push away the feathers with your fingertips; you can sew the elastic loops right to these cords.

MATERIALS

Feather boa
Pins
Fabric marker
Thread, all-purpose polyester or poly/cotton
Flat buttons, about ½ in. in diameter
Sharp hand-sewing needle, size 9
Elastic loops or ⅛-in.-wide elastic

1. If your boa is longer than the edge you want to trim, mark the appropriate length by inserting a pin temporarily into the holding cord. Part as many feathers as possible away from the

pin, and sew through the cords on both sides of it, making sure to leave space between the lines of stitches for cutting. You can use a straight machine stitch, sewing back and forth over the same area, a zigzag stitch, or sew by hand using a stab stitch (small closely spaced stitches). When you cut the boa, insert the tips of the scissors between or under as many feathers as possible and try to cut just the holding cords.

> **TIP** *If you are using the circular application, make the boa long enough so you can overlap the ends and machine- or hand-tack them together.*

2. Mark where the buttons should be placed along the garment edge. If the edge is straight, space them at even intervals, close enough to one another to preclude the boa from gapping or drooping—3 in. to 4 in. apart is usually fine. If the edge is shaped, you'll need a button at every corner or at several strategic points along a curve such as a neckline.

3. Hand-sew the buttons to the wrong side of the

garment, placing them close to the edge but so they can't be seen from the right side. Be sure the stitches do not go through to the right side of the garment so that when you wear the gar-

ment without the feathers, neither the buttons nor the stitches will be visible.

4. Next, cut individual elastic loops from the loop trim or cut 1½-in. pieces of narrow elastic and fold the elastic in half to form a loop. Align the boa with the garment edge and pin it in place temporarily. Use a pin to mark a spot for a loop on the boa opposite each button; push the feathers away from the holding cord with your fingertips for each.

> **TIP** *If your buttons are sewn on at regular intervals, you don't have to pin the boa to the garment—just measure and mark corresponding loop positions on the boa.*

5. Unpin the boa from your garment, and sew a loop at each pin mark. Move as many feathers as possible away at each point and tack each loop to the cord using a machine straight stitch or zigzag stitch, or stitch by hand.

DESIGNER IDEA

Use small boa pieces of less than 1 in. long to add fluffy feather poofs to a sweater or T-shirt. Scatter the poofs along the upper front and back, including the shoulder area. Follow the directions in step 1 at left for fastening the ends of the cord when you cut the boa. Then tack the poofs to the garment by hand or machine, or secure them using tiny brass safety pins on the inside of the garment.

Fabrics

When you're looking for materials with which to embellish a garment, you might at first overlook fabric. But the diverse world of fabric offers many decorative possibilities—appliqués, ruffles, and collage treatment can all be worked in any number of prints, weaves, textures, and finishes, each of which lends its own character to the effect. If you sew, go through your scrap bag to find bits you loved too much to toss. If you collect vintage linens, take them out of the drawer and add their printed or lacy borders to a very contemporary skirt or shirt. Or search the remnant basket at a fabric shop to find small and affordable cuts of new cloth.

Appliqués

An appliqué is any material that is cut into a shape and sewn, embroidered, or otherwise fastened to a garment. The results can be remarkably different depending on how you develop and carry out the process.

The beauty of appliqué is that it is appropriate anywhere on a garment. If you want to do just a little embellishing, you can concentrate your efforts on areas that are noticed first, such as at the front of a garment near the neck, chest, and shoulder area.

When you want to do more, and I hope you do, you can expand the radius of the design. You can't go wrong with placement if you concentrate on parts of the garment that flatter you and avoid parts that don't.

Classic fabric appliqués

The classic appliqué method entails stitching the edge of the appliqué motif in place using a satin stitch. The satin stitch covers the raw appliqué edges and outlines the shape of the motif. To vary the effect,

You can make classic appliqué more interesting by combining fabrics with different prints and textures and by using pretty threads. Here a medium-wide zigzag stitch gives a bold edge to the floral cutout.

APPLIQUÉ COMBINATIONS

You can enrich your design by your choice of fabrics. Printed fabrics are a wonderful place to start because there is a wealth of beautiful prints at your local fabric store. With printed fabric, you can cut out your appliqué shapes following the designs on the fabric and create a complex dimensional motif that looks like it is painted onto the garment. Solid-color fabrics also make wonderful appliqués. Here are some prescriptions for effective appliqué combinations:

Solid appliqué	Use on a solid garment
Print	Use on a solid or print garment
Textured fabric	Use on a smooth garment
Napped fabric	Use on anything
Leather	Use on anything
Ultrasuede®, Ultraleather	Use on anything
Sheer fabric	Use on anything

you can experiment with machine embroidery and utility stitches. Some of my favorite stitches include the feather stitch and various edging stitches that have an appealing hand-sewn look. Using specialty embroidery threads also enhances the design.

Since there are so many diverse fabrics at your local fabric store, you have many choices for appliqué embellishments. With so many colors, weights, and textures at hand, be sure to take your garment with you to the fabric store so you can choose the best combination.

You can follow a motif printed on your fabric or draw your own.

MATERIALS

Stabilizer, water soluble or tearaway, optional (see the sidebar on p. 75)
Paper-backed fusible web such as Wonder-Under®
Woven or stable knitted fabric
Embroidery foot
Thread, machine embroidery or all-purpose
Embroidery hoop, optional

1. If you want to draw your own designs, mark them on the paper side of the fusible web. Remember the designs will be reversed when the appliqués are turned right side up.

2. Stabilize the appliqué fabrics using the fusible web. To do this, place your fabric wrong side up on your ironing board, place the fusible web paper side up on top of it, and press with a dry iron, holding the iron in place for five seconds. If you want to use the motifs printed on the fabric, be sure the web is covering them.

3. Once the fabric has cooled, cut out the appliqués. If you drew your own motifs, cut through the paper and peel it off. If you are following the printed motifs, peel away the

paper backing first and then cut out the appliqués.

4. Pin the appliqués where you want them on the garment, being sure to place them web side down. Set your iron to the coolest steam setting. Fuse the

appliqués to the garment one at a time by removing the pins and then holding the iron over the appliqué for 10 seconds.

You can use appliqués to embellish just about any place on a garment.

Even very basic appliqué designs look charming when you mix patterns. Use floral prints with plaids, checks, or polka dots, then use a colorful stitching line to tie it all together.

If a blouse or a dress has an open neckline, you can add color and an organic shape to the neckline edge by positioning appliqué motifs so they overlap the neck edge. This works nicely with floral and leaf shapes as well as geometric shapes. Start by interfacing the appliqué fabric with fusible tricot interfacing, then satin stitching around the motif shape. Cut out the motif next to the satin stitching, and attach it to the neckline using a straight stitch just inside the satin stitch.

Appliqué near the collar points of a classic cotton shirt. You can select appliqué colors that tie the shirt to skirts and pants that you like to wear with the shirt. Sometimes you can snip small pieces of fabric away from the skirt or pants hem allowance to use as part of the appliqué material.

Make side slits and shirttails prettier by positioning appliqués at the corners or curves.

Jazz up a solid-color cotton shirt or top by appliquéing clear plastic circles randomly on the body. The circles will be the same color as the blouse but look wet. It is important to make the circles a bold size (about 1½ in. in diameter) so that they are large enough to stand out but not so large that they interfere with the fabric's drape. Use a zigzag stitch, a decorative edging, or just a plain straight stitch to sew the circles in place.

TIP *When applying appliqués, be sure to use a press cloth so you don't scorch the appliqué or the garment.*

5. To sew each appliqué to the garment, first choose a decorative stitch. A tight satin stitch is always appropriate, but you can also use something fancier if you like. Using an embroidery foot, sew along the perimeter of each appliqué, stitching over the cut edge. Start and end neatly using a knot stitch or sewing in place using a straight stitch. Clip all thread ends close to the fabric.

Leather or Ultrasuede appliqués

Because real or synthetic leather and Ultrasuede don't fray, they make beautiful appliqués that can be stitched to a garment using a straight stitch or zigzag stitch. Unlike fabric appliqués, a leather appliqué should be roughly cut out with a border left around its perimeter, sewn onto the garment, and then trimmed close to the stitching line—this allows you to pin the appliqué through the border so you don't mar it with permanent pin marks. However, if you'd like a casual or whimsical effect, cut appliqués to their finished size, pin minimally near the edges, and then whipstitch to the garment by hand using embroidery floss or thin ribbon.

Some special equipment makes sewing leather easier. A presser foot with a Teflon® coating will help the leather feed smoothly through the machine. If you are sewing real leather, use a leather needle, which has a sharp, three-sided point that actually slices the leather as it pierces it, to avoid skipped stitches. (The hand-sewer's version of a leather needle is called a glover's needle.) If you are sewing Ultrasuede, use a ballpoint needle. A pair of appliqué scissors is very helpful. Appliqué scissors curve up at the points, making them easier to slide between the appliqué

USING STABILIZER

I f your garment fabric is lightweight, soft, or stretches easily, you should reinforce it with a stabilizer so that it doesn't become stretched or distorted when you sew on the appliqués. Use a temporary stabilizer—both fusible tearaway and water-soluble types will work—and place it behind the entire appliqué area. After you finish embellishing, you can easily remove the stabilizer by tearing it away next to the appliqué stitches or by washing it away with water. Follow the manufacturer's directions to use whichever stabilizer you choose.

On some applications, it's not clear if additional stabilizer is necessary. You can either use the stabilizer anyway or do a test seam. Since I don't like to bother using stabilizer unless it is needed, I prefer to test the technique on a swatch of fabric with a similar weight and drape as the garment fabric. Doing so is time well spent and is good practice for sewing the actual appliqué to the garment.

The density of the stitch you use also affects the need for additional stabilizer. If you use too many stitches per inch, the appliqué stitching line will stretch. Sometimes increasing the stitch length just a bit, therefore decreasing the density of the stitch, is all it takes to reduce stretching the appliqué area.

and garment and preventing mishaps when you cut away the excess leather.

You may need to use a stabilizer to reinforce the portion of the garment behind an appliqué (see the sidebar at left). If you use a water-soluble stabilizer, be careful not to wet the leather when you remove the stabilizer. Organza is a good alternative.

TIP *You can bond Ultrasuede to paper-backed fusible web and then cut and apply it just as a fabric appliqué (see pp. 72–74). If you want to use Ultrasuede appliqués on garments that can be easily damaged by fusing or pressing such as sweaters or garments containing acrylic fibers or any garments that say "do not press" on the care label, then you should follow the directions given on the facing page for leather appliqués.*

Leather and Ultrasuede appliqués look dramatic yet are easy to do. They don't require special stitches since they do not fray.

MATERIALS

Water-soluble stabilizer or organza, optional
Air-erasable marker or chalk-wheel marker
Real or synthetic leather or Ultrasuede
Teflon-coated presser foot
Leather needle or ballpoint needle
Thread, 100% polyester
Appliqué scissors

1. Using a marker or chalk wheel, draw the appliqué shape on the leather, then cut out the shape, leaving a small border all around.

2. Pin the appliqués where you want them on the garment, being sure to place the pins in the border.

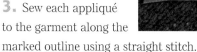

3. Sew each appliqué to the garment along the marked outline using a straight stitch.

4. Remove the pins and trim away the excess leather next to the stitching line using appliqué scissors.

Unstructured appliqués

Unstructured appliqué is less inhibited than standard appliqué and lets you sew outside of the box if you are so inclined. Instead of using a solid stitch around the edge of each appliqué motif, the line of stitches can dance across, around, and over the appliqué edges.

When you sew on the appliqués, you can use a standard presser foot and keep the feed dogs engaged as you would for classic appliqué. But you can alternatively use a darning foot and drop the feed dogs, which will allow you to easily make meandering lines of stitches and even sew in circles. This manner of stitching is called free-motion embroidery.

Depending on how much stitching you do and the type of fabric you use, you can expect the appliqué to fray somewhat with each washing, but that is part of the fun. Specialty threads are not a necessity but can help you create interesting design effects. Machine-embroidery thread is available in shiny, variegated, or metallic finishes to name a few options. Be sure to use a needle appropriate for any specialty thread you choose.

MATERIALS

Fabric
Thread, all-purpose or machine embroidery
Presser foot, standard or darning
Needle, universal point or as appropriate
 for thread

1. Cut out the desired appliqué shapes from the fabric, then arrange and pin them in place on the right side of the garment.

2. To stitch the appliqués in place, use a straight stitch but zigzag back and forth across the surface and perhaps over and past the appliqué edges. Start and end neatly by using a knot stitch or by sewing in place using a straight stitch. When you are done, either cut the threads or pull them to the back and tie them together.

Unstructured appliqué is fancy free—you place the motifs wherever you wish and then sew over them in random directions, without regard for their edges. I like to run the stitches from one shape to another.

Handkerchief appliqués

For an easy, perky hem, appliqué handkerchief godets around the bottom of a skirt. In dressmaking, godets are flared pieces inserted to add fullness between two straight panels, typically of a skirt. They're generally wedge-shaped, but they can be quarter-round or even semicircular. You can create a godet effect by applying wedge-shaped pieces on top of a skirt, positioning each with the pointed end toward the waistline and bringing the straight sides close together so the wedge itself lifts away from the skirt, fluting out at the hemline.

Choose handkerchiefs with pretty embroidered corners, monograms, or vintage printed motifs. They can be all the same or assorted. The number you need depends on the skirt, the size of the handkerchief, and the effect you want to create—use the photo at right as a guide.

You'll need to hem the wide edge of each wedge, so plan how you'll do this ahead of time so you include the appropriate seam allowance.

MATERIALS

Handkerchiefs, one for each godet
Thread, all-purpose

1. Cut a quarter-round wedge from one corner of each handkerchief. Using a ruler or compass, mark a quarter-circle with a radius of 5 in. to 8 in. from the corner point (you'll need to finish the curved edge, so include a hem allowance).

2. Finish the curved edge of each wedge by zigzagging, serging, or machine-sewing a narrow hem. To sew a narrow hem, staystitch the curved edge using a ¼-in. seam allowance, then press back the hem allowance

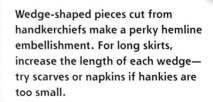

Wedge-shaped pieces cut from handkerchiefs make a perky hemline embellishment. For long skirts, increase the length of each wedge— try scarves or napkins if hankies are too small.

along the stitching line. Stitch again ¹⁄₁₆ in. to ⅛ in. from the fold, then carefully trim the hem allowance next to the stitching.

3. Next, arrange the wedges around the lower edge of the skirt. Orient the points toward the waistline, spacing them evenly or as desired, and pin in place. Then bring the straight edges of each wedge toward

one another so the godet lifts from the surface of the skirt, aligning the lower end of each side edge with the lower edge of the skirt. Check that the handkerchief edges are smooth; you may need to remove the pin at the point and move the point up a bit. Pin the sides of each godet to the skirt.

4. Sew the sides of each godet to the skirt using a straight stitch or small zigzag stitch.

Decorative hidden closures

Try this unexpected use of appliqué to conceal an ordinary button closure. It's easy to add this decorative placket, and since it isn't attached right at the garment edge, you will still be able to fasten the buttons.

In a nutshell, the placket is simply a folded length of fabric stitched over the buttonholes. The folded edge of the placket aligns with the edge of the garment; the opposite edge of the placket can be straight or cut in a decorative or geometric pattern.

Choose a fabric with a print you can follow to create a shaped placket, or draw an edge shaped in a way you like on any fabric that pleases you. You can

Turn a conventional button closure into a covered placket by applying a shaped band of contrasting fabric. Use additional fabric to trim the collar, cuffs, or pockets.

use all-purpose thread or a machine-embroidery thread to appliqué the placket; choose whichever works for your garment and fabric. If you go with machine-embroidery thread, be sure to use bobbin/lingerie thread in the bobbin.

MATERIALS

Fabric
Lightweight fusible interfacing
Presser feet, standard and machine embroidery
Thread, all-purpose, or machine embroidery
 and bobbin/lingerie
Appliqué scissors

1. To use a printed fabric for the placket, choose a motif. With the right side out, fold the fabric so that the motif is oriented the

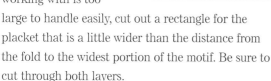

way you want when you align the fold with the edge of the buttonhole portion of the garment.

2. Press the fold. If the fabric piece you're working with is too large to handle easily, cut out a rectangle for the placket that is a little wider than the distance from the fold to the widest portion of the motif. Be sure to cut through both layers.

3. Next, cut a piece of fusible interfacing the same size as the folded rectangle. Unfold the rectangle and fuse the interfacing to the wrong side of the half with the motif (the half that faces out when you wear the garment). With the right side out, refold the rectangle and press.

4. Position and pin the placket on the garment, covering the buttonholes as planned and aligning the fold with the garment edge. Using a standard presser foot and

a straight stitch, sew the placket to the garment along the edge of the motif.

5. Cut away the excess border fabric next to the stitching line using appliqué scissors.

6. Using an embroidery foot, sew a zigzag or satin stitch over the straight stitch, making sure to cover the edges of the placket.

Tulle Collage

Tulle, also called illusion, can be used to create interesting embellishments on garments. Because it is crisp, transparent, and available in a wide range of colors, tulle is a fabric with lots of decorative potential.

The transparent colors take on the color of the garment you are embellishing, so you can use it as a nearly invisible barrier that holds other embellishment materials in place on the garment. For example, you can cut out small sections of tulle and sew them onto the garment like pockets, filling them with tiny treasures. You also can use tulle to create easy collages that incorporate yarns, fabrics, buttons, trims, and glitter. You can further embellish and topstitch these collages using all-purpose, specialty, or machine-embroidery thread.

Collage designs can be added to any accessible area of a garment, but they are especially nice to use on yokes and hems. Remember that you can include small pieces of fabrics and trims that, because of their size, would be completely unusable in conventional sewing.

Use the following basic collage technique to embellish selective areas of the garment, or use the second technique to create collage designs that extend past the garment edges and seem to float in space.

Basic collage

This simple method can be used to decorate small or large sections of any jacket, sweatshirt, or shirt. To begin, gather a selection of trims and trinkets—anything from yarn to buttons. After arranging the embellishment materials on the garment, you'll cover them with a layer of tulle, which serves as an invisible barrier that holds everything in place.

To sew on the tulle, use a darning foot and drop the feed dogs, which will allow you to easily make meandering lines of stitches and even sew in circles. With the tulle layer as security, you won't have to sew every single trinket or thread individually. It's important to select washable embellishment materials for washable garments and dry-cleanable materials for dry-clean-only garments. And be smart: Don't try to sew over buttons or other rigid trinkets.

MATERIALS

Air-erasable marker
Stabilizer
Temporary spray adhesive
Embellishment materials
Tulle, illusion or fishnet
Thread, all-purpose or machine embroidery
Darning foot

To transform a plain garment into an artful collage, layer tulle strips or squares on a garment, then float trinkets or pretty scraps behind them. Secure the loose items by stitching the tulle to the garment so that a loose grid, or series of pockets, forms around them.

Tulle pockets can hold all manner of whimsical and decorative materials. I love the way the tulle masks the trinkets and lets them float within small, defined spaces.

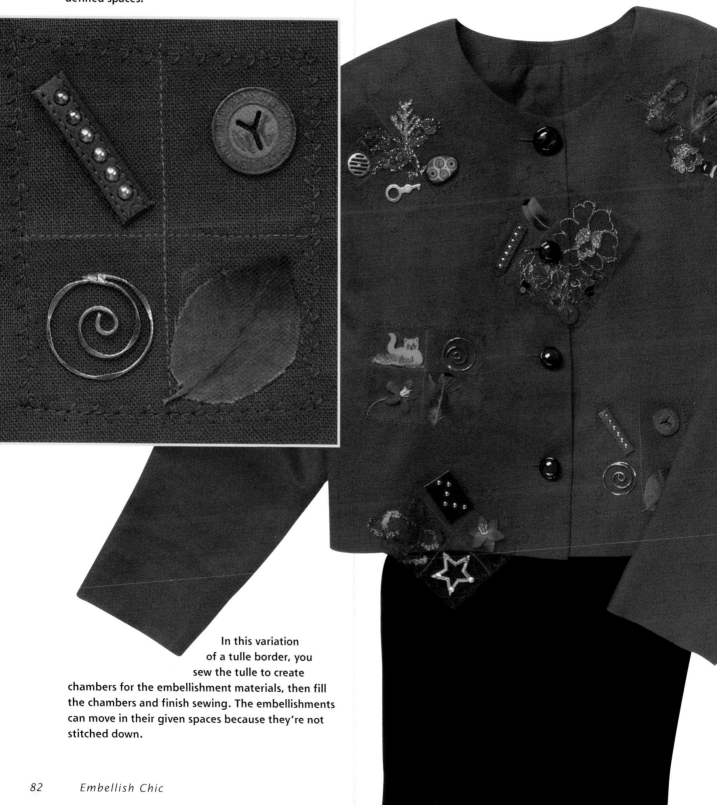

In this variation of a tulle border, you sew the tulle to create chambers for the embellishment materials, then fill the chambers and finish sewing. The embellishments can move in their given spaces because they're not stitched down.

1. Define the design area on the garment by drawing lines using an air-erasable marker or by machine-basting. For example, if the collage will be about 4 in. wide and placed along the hem of a skirt, you need one line 4 in. above the hem edge. If you want to start the same collage 1 in. above the hem, then place one line 1 in. above the hem and a second line 4 in. above the first. All of the embellishment components don't need to line up with the line. Use the line as the outside edge of all materials.

2. When working with lightweight garments, pin, baste, or fuse the stabilizer behind the embellishment area on the wrong side of the garment.

TIP Although I've used a border as an example for defining the collage space, keep in mind that the shape of the collage can be any size or shape that you would like it to be as long as the area is accessible for sewing by machine. The little collage pockets decorating the orange jacket shown in the photo at left are made in the same manner; they're just smaller.

3. Using temporary spray adhesive, spray the embellishment area and arrange the embellishment materials on the garment.

4. Cut one or two strips of tulle a few inches wider and longer than the collage area, then position the tulle to cover the collage design and pin it to the garment.

5. Machine-stitch the tulle and the decorative materials in place using free-motion embroidery. Sew back and forth or meander around through all the layers.

TIP The more stitches you use, the stiffer the collage becomes, so limit the amount of stitching if you want to keep things soft, but stitch away with abandon if you want to add structure or body to the area.

DESIGNER IDEA

Adding a collage border along both sides of the front opening on a cardigan sweater or simple jacket will get you rave reviews every time you wear it. This is a great way to tie a sweater or jacket into other things that you like to wear it with. Take small snips from inside the hems of those other garments and use the snips as part of the collage design. If the garments are of a solid color, you can buy a small amount of fabric in the same color (it doesn't have to be the same fabric) so that you'll have larger and more prominent pieces of fabric to work with within the collage design.

Floating collage hems

Like magic, you can suspend a collage design in space (or more precisely, off the edge of a garment) by sandwiching the embellishment material between two layers of tulle. This technique is easiest to use along a straight edge, but if you are a confident sewer you will soon figure out that it is also possible to use on shaped edges as well. It just takes more skill.

It is best to embellish the border before attaching it to the garment. The collage is more manageable if you don't have to manipulate the garment as you sew.

Because tulle is very lightweight and fine, use fine machine-embroidery thread, such as 60/2-ply machine-embroidery thread or Sulky® rayon embroidery thread, to stitch the layers together. Use an embroidery hoop, or frame the tulle and interfacing with your hands to help keep things smooth.

MATERIALS

Stabilizer, water soluble
Fabric marker
Tulle, illusion or fishnet
Temporary spray adhesive
Embellishment materials
Thread, fine embroidery
Embroidery hoop, optional
Standard presser foot

1. Measure the garment edge to figure the length of the finished collage, and decide how deep you want the border to be.

2. Cut a rectangle of water-soluble stabilizer 1 in. deeper and 2 in. longer than the finished border. (Be sure to use a ruler to mark straight cutting lines.)

3. Using a fabric marker, draw a line 1 in. away from one long edge to define the top sewing line,

which you'll use to align the collage with the garment edge. Fold the stabilizer in half crosswise, and mark the center point using a pencil or fabric marker. If you are making a border for the bottom of a skirt, it is also useful to mark the side seams to give you some guidelines for arranging the embellishments.

4. Fold the tulle so that you can cover the stabilizer with a double layer, aligning the fold with one long

edge of the stabilizer. Pin the tulle to the stabilizer, then cut it out using the stabilizer as a pattern.

5. Unfold the tulle so only one layer covers the stabilizer and the excess extends off the unmarked edge of the stabilizer. Pin or baste the top edges together.

6. To prepare for spraying adhesive on the tulle collage area, cover your work surface with paper. Spray the portion of tulle that covers the stabilizer with the adhesive. Position the embellishment materials on the tulle border, being sure to confine the design to the

A collaged tulle border extending below the hem completely changes the design sensibility of a garment. Subtle colors and enclosed embellishments give this classic dress a chic modern edge.

stabilized area; don't extend the design above the line marking the top edge.

7. Once the design is complete, fold up the remaining tulle along the edge of the stabilizer to cover the embellishment material.

8. Baste the tulle to the stabilizer ¾ in. from the top cut edge, then place the border in an embroidery hoop or plan to frame it with your hands when you sew. Using a standard presser foot, machine-stitch the tulle and the decorative materials in place. Sew back and forth or meander around through all of the layers.

9. Measure the length of the border, compare it with the garment edge, and mark the correct length on the border, leaving a seam allowance at each end. If this is a circular application, overlap the ends and sew the tulle together using a narrow to medium zigzag stitch. Otherwise, turn back the tulle on the marked line and zigzag near the fold.

10. Cut off the excess tulle, leaving a ¼-in. seam allowance next to the zigzag stitch.

11. Remove the water-soluble stabilizer by wetting the border, then allow the border to dry.

12. Position and pin the tulle border under the garment edge, aligning the marked line with the garment edge and the center and any side seam marks as appropriate. (If the old line is

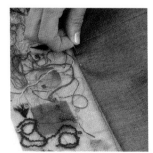

no longer visible, draw a new one.) Sew the border in place by machine, topstitching as close as possible to the garment edge, or sew invisibly by hand along the edge.

TIP *To move the embroidery hoop without interrupting the stitching, stop sewing near the hoop perimeter with the needle in the fabric and the presser foot down, and unfasten the hoop from the garment. Reposition the hoop to include the adjacent section of the design and continue sewing.*

Borders

You can use fabric borders to create bold, beautiful edges. They can outline a neckline, front opening, or hemline. Take advantage of border prints and striped fabrics, or make a "cutwork" border from a solid fabric.

Border prints

The nice thing about border prints cut from yardage is the ease with which they can add an element of surprise or drama to plain garments. Picture a pinstriped skirt with a paisley, floral, or geometric printed border design at the hemline or a wrap skirt with a colorful border along the front edge. The borders easily align with straight edges anywhere on a garment. Look for printed fabrics with one or more border designs, or select an allover printed fabric. Striped fabrics also make nice borders that can be used with the stripes following the edge or running perpendicular to it.

I dressed up this basic linen skirt by adding a border cut from a printed fabric. To make the design even more interesting, I worked a pattern of cutwork squares above the border, then sewed the cutouts to the skirt as unstructured appliqués.

Does the border design need to be centered? Most border prints have horizontal designs that have an overall effect. Look over the border design to see if any part of the design stands out more than another. Borders with prominent motifs and up-and-down scalloped effects should be centered. In this case, cut the borders several inches longer than you need, then center a dominant motif at the center of the garment edge.

Borders seem to be made to be used on hems. Hem applications are the easiest and most straightforward, and you have several easy placement options. You can position the border so that the lower edge ends at the hemline, a little below the hemline, or several inches below the hemline of the garment (this is a decorative way to lengthen the garment). Or you can position the border to end above the hem of the garment and leave the lower edge unstitched to create a nice, tiered effect.

Because borders are straight, you will get the best results if you select garments with straight hemlines. Otherwise the straight border will restrict the lower edge of the garment.

Since hem applications are horizontal, I prefer to connect just the upper edge of the border design to the garment because it's faster and results in a softer finish.

MATERIALS

Border-print fabric
Stabilizer, fusible tearaway or permanent, optional (see the sidebar on p. 75)
Thread, all-purpose or as appropriate
Paper-backed fusible web

1. Measure the garment edge to figure the length of the finished border, and decide how deep you want the border to be. Cut the border 2 in. wider and 2 in. deeper than the finished size.

2. Finish the lower edge of the border. If the edge is straight, simply hem it. If you want it to follow a printed motif, reinforce the motif area with a strip of stabilizer, then sew a straight stitch along the motif edge. Cut away the excess fabric, and finish the cut edge with a satin stitch.

3. To prepare the top edge of the border, fuse a strip of paper-backed fusible web to the wrong side

of the upper edge. If you want the edge to follow a printed motif, be sure the strip is under the motif.

4. If appropriate, cut away the excess fabric at the top of the border to follow the motif. Overlap the top edge of the border on the right side of the garment edge and pin. Fuse in place, being sure to remove the pins from the area you are fusing. Using a straight stitch, sew

the upper edge of the border to the garment, then sew along the edge again using a satin stitch or a decorative embroidery stitch.

A complex-looking applied border such as this lattice is easy to set up when you use a fold-and-cut pattern—it's as easy as making paper dolls.

Add-on cutout borders

Try adding decorative border motifs that let the garment fabric peek through the border design. These intricate-looking borders are easy to do—they're actually similar to making paper-doll cutouts, but the results are more sophisticated. Before you begin, make a rough sketch of the border design you want so you understand how to repeat it around your garment. You'll make a template for one portion of the garment, fold and cut it as you would for paper dolls,

and unfold it to use as a pattern. By using this template, you can make a repeating pattern without spending a lot of time on math.

Ultrasuede and jersey are my favorite fabrics for this technique because they look great, are soft and pliable, and won't fray when stitched in place with a simple straight stitch or a medium zigzag stitch. Be sure to use a needle designed for stretch fabrics if you choose Ultrasuede, but you can use an all-purpose needle with jersey. Use 100% polyester thread with Ultrasuede.

MATERIALS

Brown paper
Fabric
Paper-backed fusible web
Temporary spray adhesive, optional
Air-erasable fabric marker or tailor's chalk
Thread, all-purpose or as appropriate

1. To make a template, cut a brown-paper rectangle equal to one-half or one-quarter the width of the garment at the lower edge (hemline) and as tall as the planned motif. For example, if the hemline is 60 in., you can divide that amount by four and make a 15-in. template. My sample garment measures 38 in. around the lower edge, so I made a template half that width (19 in.).

2. Fold the paper into fourths, placing the folds perpendicular to the lower edge, then sketch a simple pattern (such as the diamond lattice on my skirt shown on p. 89). If you  place half of a motif on the folds, it will be complete once the template is unfolded. Decide which portion of the design should be removed (the remaining portion will actually be the border pattern), and cut it out through all four layers.

> **TIP** If it's been a while since you made paper dolls, try the technique of folding and cutting without necessarily having a specific design in mind just to get an idea of how a design unfolds.

> **TIP** If your pattern has interior sections, place the pattern on a cutting mat and use a craft knife to cut them out.

> **TIP** To make your garment more interesting, save the cutouts and incorporate them in the design. The separate diamonds on my skirt are just the cutout portions of the diamond lattice—I cut them again to make the diamond frames and used their centers for the small separate diamonds.

3. Lay the template over the garment and check that it repeats evenly and pleasingly all around. Be sure you understand and like the alignment of the repeats with the center front, center back, and sides of the garment. If you don't, adjust or redo the template.

4. To prepare the border fabric, first cut it into a rectangle 2 in. deeper than the border pattern and 2 in. wider than the hemline circumference. Cut a piece of paper-backed fusible the same size, then fuse the web to the wrong side of the border fabric using a dry iron. Leave the iron in place for five seconds, and peel away the paper backing when everything cools.

> **TIP** If the fabric isn't wide enough to go all around the garment, cut it in sections and sew them together before you cut and fuse the web.

5. Turn the rectangle right side up on your work surface, and place the template on top at one end. (If you want to seam the border at the center back, be sure to allow for a seam  allowance at the end.) Pin or tape the template to the fabric (or spray the back of the template with a temporary adhesive first). Outline the design lines using an air-erasable marker or tailor's chalk.

6. For the next repeat, reposition the template and mark again, then do the same for each remaining repeat. Cut out the border along the marked lines, saving the cutouts if you would like to further embellish the garment.

7. Sew the center back seam if you allowed for it.

8. Pin the border to your garment, positioning the repeat as planned. Using a steam setting on an iron and a press cloth, lightly press the lower edge of the border at the center front of the garment to just hold the border in place. Check the fit all around, then fuse the entire border.

9. Finally, sew the edges of the border to the garment. For Ultrasuede or jersey, you can use a straight stitch or a medium zigzag that's 2mm wide and long. For fabrics more likely to fray, use a satin stitch or decorative embroidery stitch.

DESIGNER IDEA

Instead of using one bold add-on border, select three or more complementary shades of Ultrasuede or wool jersey to make several smaller bands that embellish the hem. Each band could have simple but different cutout motifs such as squares, triangles, or diamonds. Varying the depth of each band is more interesting than making all the bands the same depth. Follow the basic technique on p. 89 to space the cutouts so they fit the garment perfectly without having to do the math.

Use add-on cutout borders over collars or cuffs, or along the shoulder line of a top or sweater, to create a decorative yoke effect.

Add interest to the entire front of a shirt, or any other garment with a front placket opening, by positioning the cutout border on each side of the placket. You can run the design down the entire length of the front opening or just part of the way to create a bib effect. The removed motifs can then be used to embellish the placket or to expand the design toward each side seam.

Take add-on borders a step further by mitering the border to follow corners—for instance, on a garment with side slits or along the flange of a square or rectangular pillow cover.

A bias-cut skirt or top makes an excellent canvas for add-on borders. If you position them diagonally so that they follow the fabric grain, they will be both easy to sew and flattering on the body. Position one or more borders to form a V or chevron effect at the front and back, or just place them diagonally so they miter at the sides of the garment.

Hardware

Easy-to-find metal embellishments such as zippers, grommets, and nail heads are fun to use because the results can be so varied. Although these embellishments are typically associated with biker-chick and punk accessories, you can also use metal accents to make basic garments more individual and to counterbalance soft-and-sweet or ladylike garments with an urban edge.

Zipper Teeth

Forget the useful aspect of zippers and use them to add a zippy edge to necklines, collars, and hems. Brass zippers and chunky, colorful plastic separating zippers are the most fun to work with because the bold teeth really stand out along the edge of a garment.

Use zippers to enliven the edges on:

- Collars, pockets, and flaps on jackets and shirts
- Hems on tops, skirts, pants, and dresses
- Along all the outer edges of a simple jacket or vest

Zipper "piping"

In place of piping, try using zippers to accentuate the edges on sporty garments. Use brass or nickel zippers to give edges a heavy-metal appeal, or create playful edges using colorful plastic zippers. Zippers are readily available and easy to attach using each half of the zipper along the garment edge. Since metal and plastic separating zippers are stiff, use them on garments that have body or the zipper will overpower the garment. Standard zippers are lightweight and suitable for lightweight garments.

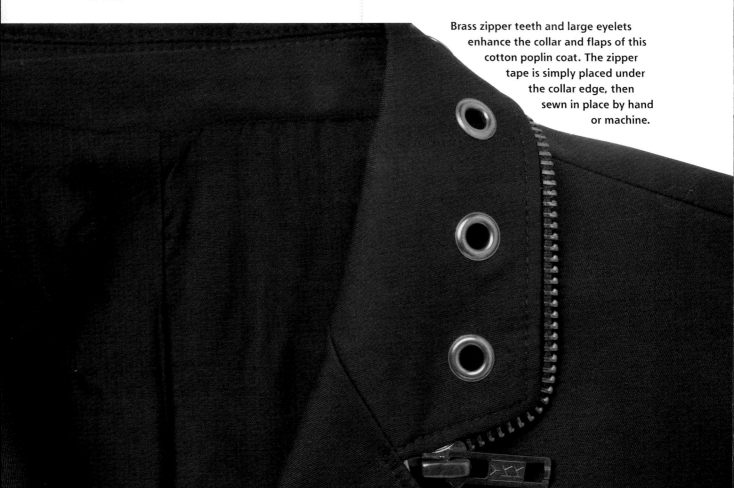

Brass zipper teeth and large eyelets enhance the collar and flaps of this cotton poplin coat. The zipper tape is simply placed under the collar edge, then sewn in place by hand or machine.

For a sporty but glittery trim, stitch a half zipper to jeans or a jacket; be sure to use a zipper foot so you can sew close to the teeth. Trim the zipper tape away next to the stitching and sew again using a zigzag stitch.

MATERIALS

Metal or plastic zipper at least 2 in.
*   longer than the edge to be*
*   trimmed*
Pliers
Zipper foot
Thread, all-purpose

1. Position and pin the zipper tape behind the garment so that the zipper teeth extend beyond the edge.

2. Once you establish the length of the zipper trim you need, remove a few teeth at each

end so that you can finish the tape ends neatly. Use pliers to pull the teeth away from the tape.

3. Cut away the excess zipper, leaving ½-in. seam allowances at each end, then fold both cut edges toward the garment. If you are applying the zipper all the way around a closed circular edge—for instance, a trouser hem or pullover neckline—allow ½ in. of excess tape at each end so the teeth will meet at the join and the tape will overlap.

4. Using a zipper foot, sew the zipper in place from the right side of the garment.

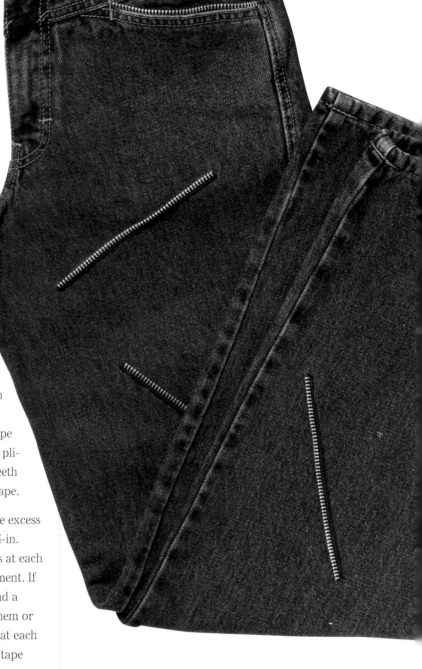

TIP *To avoid scratches on your skin or blouse, be sure to select zippers with smooth edges. This is especially important when attaching a zipper to a neckline where the teeth will lie against your skin or where it will rub against a delicate fabric.*

There are many fun ways in which you can use zippers to jazz up a garment.

- *Instead of separating the zipper, keep it intact and attach it in the open position to the wrong side of a boat neckline or V neckline. Place the zipper pull at the shoulder seam of a boat neckline or at the point of a V neckline. Adding the zipper in a permanent open position to the inside V of a notched collar makes the zipper look as though it could possibly close.*

- *Add a zippy edge to the collar of a plain jacket by positioning and stitching a heavy-gauge brass zipper so that just the teeth show along the edge of the collar and the zipper tape faces the under collar.*

- *Sew zipper halves at rakish angles randomly over a pair of jeans. To make the tape less prominent, first stitch next to the teeth, then trim the tape near the stitching and stitch again using a narrow zigzag to cover the raw edges.*

TIP *Don't use grommets or eyelets in areas that need to stretch or on very elastic knits because the hole will stretch and the eyelets will pop out of the fabric. You can use them on knits with little to moderate stretch if you first stabilize the area with fusible woven or nonwoven interfacing. Cut circles of interfacing just slightly larger than the hardware.*

To set grommets and eyelets, you'll need a cutting tool and a setting tool, which will either be included in the package of grommets or sold separately in the same section of the store. The size of the grommets

Insert grommets or eyelets along darts or seamlines. Single rows are strictly decorative, but double rows can also be laced to slightly modify the width of the garment.

Grommets and Eyelets

Grommets and eyelets have a functional use, but don't let that stop you from using them decoratively to create some spirited designs. They have a bold and sassy look.

Grommets and eyelets are available in sizes ranging from dainty to sturdy and having diameters of ⅛ in. to greater than 1 in. Most are gold or silver tone, but you occasionally see small, enameled eyelets in colors such as red, blue, and black. With the exception of a hammer or mallet, you can buy supplies at fabric stores, craft stores, or through mail-order sources.

and the tools must be compatible, just as the weight and thickness of the grommet must be compatible with the weight and thickness of the garment fabric.

Setting grommets and eyelets

Setting small or medium eyelets is straightforward: Punch a hole in the garment, then insert the eyelet and flatten the back. Grommets and large eyelets are secured with a washer on the back. The washer creates a neat and more finished edge and reinforces the hole. To set grommets and eyelets, you'll need a special punch and die, which are sized to correspond to the grommet and eyelet sizes; large grommet setters also include a cupped base.

Small eyelets can be applied using a plierlike tool, which will punch the holes and set the eyelets. However, plierlike setters can only be used if you are attaching eyelets near the edge of a garment because their jaws are too short to accommodate much fabric.

MATERIALS

Fabric marker or pencil
Wooden cutting block or a thick stack
  of newspaper
Hole cutter, plier type or die cutter
Mallet or hammer if using die tools
Eyelets or grommets
Setting tool, plier type or die setter and base

1. Mark the eyelet/grommet placement using a fabric marker or pencil, then put the cutting block or newspaper under the mark. Place the cutter over the mark, and strike it with a mallet or hammer to cut each hole.

2. Insert the eyelet/grommet shaft through the hole from the right side of the garment, and place the garment on your work surface with the eyelet/grommet side down. If the eyelet/grommet requires a washer, slip it, rounded side up, over the shaft.

3. For small eyelets, insert the setting tool into the center of the shaft, and strike the tool with the mallet until the shaft flattens and spreads over the cut fabric edge. For eyelets/grommets

with washers, slide the setting base under the garment until it cups an eyelet/grommet, insert the setter into the center of the shaft, and strike the setter with the mallet or hammer until the shaft flattens and spreads over the washer.

TIP *Practice setting eyelets and grommets on fabric that has the same thickness as the garment you plan to embellish to get used to the tools and to be sure that you like the results.*

DESIGNER IDEA

Grommets and eyelets can be arranged in myriad decorative ways.

• *Use grommets and eyelets to make a decorative and finished path, particularly along necklines, hemlines, and edges, then weave a trim or a cord through them like a drawstring or whip the trim through the grommets and over the edge.*

• *Grommets and eyelets can appear in any area on garments or accessories. Try placing the grommets randomly to create a Swiss-cheese effect over entire items, such as shirts, tops, dresses, vests, skirts, pants, purses, totes, belts, hats, and gloves, or on selected sections of the garment, such as collars, cuffs, and pockets.*

• *Combine different-sized grommets and eyelets on the same project. Or use a more systematic approach by placing the grommets along a marked design to create openwork borders or patterned designs within the garment.*

Quick fringe

Here's an incredibly easy way to add fringe to a scarf, stole, hemline, or neckline. Just set large eyelets along the edge at regular intervals, then cut ribbon or yarn into pieces 2½ to 3 times the desired fringe depth. Fold the strands in half, singly or in small groups, pass the fold through an eyelet to create a loop, and slip the ends through the loop. Pull the ends to tighten the loop. Experiment with your ribbons to find the right proportions before cutting too many pieces.

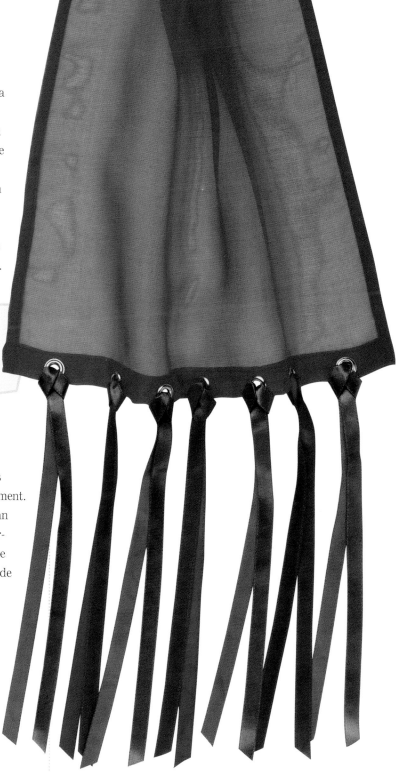

DESIGNER IDEA

To create a scalloped effect, place grommets halfway off an edge. Add fringe if you like.

Lace-up closures

Use a lace-up closure to add a fun and perhaps risque trim to T-shirts or any tight, pull-on garment. (If you sew your own clothing, of course you can incorporate this finish into any close-fitting garment.) To reinforce the opening and support the eyelets, you can apply a ribbon band to each side and set the eyelets into it.

You'll need ribbon equal to twice the length of the garment opening (plus extra for turning under) and wide enough to support the eyelets you've chosen. Once you've read "Setting Grommets and Eyelets" on p. 97 and understand the basic technique, the following is all you need to do.

MATERIALS

Grosgrain or other ribbon
Thread, all-purpose
Eyelets or grommets
Punch and setter
Cord or ribbon for lacing

For a clever way to fringe garments, scarves, and accessories, add eyelets or grommets along an edge, then loop a length of ribbon, fine cord, yarn, or a strip of Ultrasuede or leather through each.

1. Start by cutting the garment to create the opening, from neck to hem or waist to hem as appropriate.

2. Cut the ribbon in half crosswise. Place the garment  right side up and position one piece of ribbon along each side of the opening, aligning the ribbon so it just covers the cut edge. Pin the ribbon in place, turning under the ends.

3. Using a zigzag or straight stitch, sew all edges of the ribbon to the garment.

4. Measure and mark the eyelet positions, spacing them however seems best, then apply the eyelets using the punch and setter.

5. Thread the lacing cord loosely through the eyelets—you'll adjust it once you put the garment on.

DESIGNER **IDEA**

Try cutting a T-shirt horizontally, all the way around the midriff or hips. Apply ribbon and eyelets to each cut edge, then lace the top to the bottom.

If you want to dress up a sleek pair of jeans or a miniskirt, add large grommets or eyelets to the upper edge. Weave a chain belt or ribbon through the grommets when you're in the mood.

Convert a pullover tank into a lace-up vest using grosgrain ribbon and eyelets or grommets. I stitched two patterned ribbons together to make a decorative lacing; decorative shoelaces and cords also work nicely.

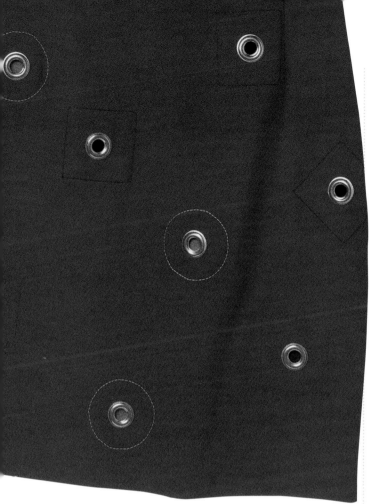

Large, grommet-bound windows filled with contrasting fabric give a surprisingly sophisticated flair to a plain garment.

Adding color with grommets

Add windows of color to a garment by decorating it with large grommets and placing a contrasting fabric piece behind each. You can position the grommets randomly or create an orderly pattern, for instance at a hemline. You'll be topstitching 1 in. to 2 in. outside each grommet, so plan the spacing with that in mind.

Be sure to cut the fabric into generous pieces—4 in. to 5 in. square—so you'll have no trouble securing them by stitching from the right side of the garment. For the topstitching, you can use either one strand of topstitching thread in the needle or two strands of all-purpose thread. Use all-purpose thread in the bobbin. Read "Setting Grommets and Eyelets" on p. 97 before you begin.

MATERIALS

Large grommets
Punch and die setter
Air-erasable marker or chalk-wheel marker
Fabric for decorative inserts
Thread, all-purpose and topstitching, if desired
Machine-topstitching needle

1. Mark the placement for the grommets and attach them using the punch and die setter.

2. To mark the topstitching guides on the right side of the garment, draw a line around each grommet using an air-erasable marker or a chalk-wheel marker. Draw geometric shapes such as squares, circles, triangles, diamonds, or free-form contour shapes.

3. Position a contrasting fabric piece behind each grommet, and pin or baste in place from the right side.

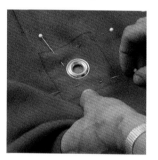

4. Using a 3mm to 4mm stitch length depending on the thickness of the layers, topstitch along each marked line. To end neatly, sew in place for three stitches, then pull all the threads to the back and tie them together.

DESIGNER IDEA

Hardware touches are perfect on leather and canvas. Embellish the sides of a tote bag with grommets, eyelets, and studs in a variety of shapes and sizes to create a tote bag worthy of a modern urban gladiator.

Nail Heads and Studs

Nail heads and studs are add-on metal shapes that are strictly decorative. You'll find them in a selection of shapes, sizes, and contours, but round and square shapes are the most common. They are easy to apply anywhere on a garment because they have prongs that you can just poke through the fabric wherever you like; you then fold back the prongs to grip the fabric by using a setting tool. For best results, select garments made from stable fabric that is not easily snagged. Nail heads and studs are difficult to use on heavy fabrics because the prongs are too short to fold back in a secure grip.

Setting nail heads

Use nail heads and studs to create fancy collar or cuff effects, to decorate pocket flaps, to outline garment details, or to create a pattern on a plain fabric. It's a good idea to plan the pattern you want to create—the nail heads are easy to apply but sometimes difficult to remove without damaging the fabric.

MATERIALS

Nail heads
Thick towel
Setter or spoon handle

1. Mark the nail-head placement on the right side of the garment.

2. Push the nail-head prongs gently through the fabric from the right side of the garment.

3. Padding your work surface with a towel so the nail heads won't get scratched, turn the garment wrong side up on the towel and flatten the prongs using a setter or the handle of a spoon.

DESIGNER IDEA

Randomly space nail heads and studs over entire garments such as vests, skirts, and pants; accessories such as purses, totes, belts, hats, gloves, and shoes; and to embellish collars, cuffs, pockets, and plackets.

Draw simple shapes such as diamond patterns, circles, and swirls on a garment, and apply nail heads, rivets, or studs following those designs. Try combining different sizes and shapes on the same project, or combine with eyelets or rhinestones.

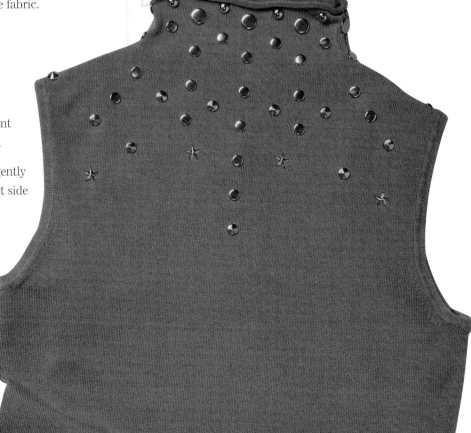

This funnel-neck silk sweater proves nail-head trim can enhance without hardening—there's nothing punky or tough about this treatment.

Threads

Thread embellishments are versatile and use the simplest and most commonplace materials—just threads and yarns of all sizes and your sewing machine. A simple machine that can zigzag is all you need, but if you have a fancier machine, you have more options with additional utility and programmed embroidery stitches. You can use machine-embroidery threads with assorted machine stitches to make your own design, to sew free-motion squiggles and swirls, and to make satin-stitch openings that further embellish a garment. Extra-thick threads can be used in the bobbin or couched in place to create linear designs that imitate crewel embroidery or to make motifs such as the chenille polka dots shown on p. 112.

Machine Embroidery

You do not need an embroidery machine to add wonderful thread embellishments to clothing. In fact, in this chapter you'll see many clever ways to do this with a classic sewing machine using both utility and simple decorative stitches. Even a basic straight-stitch machine has some capacity for embellishment if you use specialty threads in the needle, unusual threads in the bobbin, or free-motion stitching.

Start by playing with the stitches on some practice fabric. Since you will be trying out many stitch settings, it is best to keep a record of the settings you like. First, sew the stitch using the preset or standard setting, then exaggerate the widths and lengths to create stitches that closely mimic the scale of hand-sewn stitches. You probably won't like all the possible varia-tions, but when you find something you like, mark the settings right on the sample.

Then try out the decorative and utility stitches using the thread you plan to use. Try out different threads, starting with many of the wonderful machine-embroidery threads that are available at your fabric store or from mail-order sources. Also try using all-purpose threads, and don't hesitate to use many different threads on one project.

> **TIP** *You can make the stitching bolder by using two ends of thread in the needle (and one in the bobbin).*

Rows of machine-embroidery and utility stitches accent the front edge of this wrap skirt. The simple stitches look bold if you use two strands of machine-embroidery thread in the needle and only one in the bobbin.

PREPARING EMBROIDERY

I f your garment fabric is lightweight or a knit, you should use a stabilizer to support the embroidery. Choose a stabilizer that is compatible with your fabric. If the garment is washable, you can use a water-soluble stabilizer. If not, or if you prefer, use either a tearaway or permanent stabilizer, such as Fusi-Knit™ or Sof Brush, which are available at most fabric stores.

Tearaway stabilizers are good behind areas that are embellished with dense stitching. They prevent stretching and are easy to cut or tear away. My preference for most of the projects in this chapter is to use permanent fusible stabilizers because they have a nice drape and they help the area surrounding the design to stay smooth.

It is best to cut the interfacing larger than the design area in case you decide to expand the area. Lightly fuse the interfacing in place so that you can remove any excess after embellishing the garment. If possible, place the area to be embroidered in an embroidery hoop. Also, if your sewing-machine presser foot can be raised and lowered with a knee lever, this will free up your hands and make it easier to rotate the garment.

Using utility and decorative stitches

You don't need a sophisticated machine to embellish a garment with attractive embroidered patterns. With imagination, the stitches basic to all but the very simplest sewing machines can be combined with other embellishments or with one another to great effect. In fact, when used together, basic stitches—straight, various zigzags, simple decorative scallops—look far more interesting than you would think.

Use simple machine-embroidery stitches to make "trim." Here I cut buttonhole-like slashes in a sweatshirt, wove strips of sweatshirt fleece through the slashes, and enhanced and secured the strips with free-motion squiggles. Before stitching, I stabilized the embroidery area with Fusi-Knit.

For an easy embellishment, use a decorative stitch to secure an unstructured appliqué (see pp. 76–77).

A fine use of basic stitches is a deep border that follows a hemline. All you have to do is sew parallel rows, changing the stitch for each row. You can get fancier if you also change the thread—either color or type.

TIP *To keep the rows parallel, use the quilting-guide attachment on your machine. Or draw parallel lines on your garment using a transparent gridded ruler as a guide.*

Using specialty threads in the needle

Machine-embroidery threads are available in a wonderful array of finishes and fibers, each having different characteristics that can make your decorative stitches more interesting. Use the specialty threads in the needle only, and use an all-purpose sewing thread, woolly nylon, or bobbin/lingerie thread in the bobbin. Expect to loosen the needle thread, and often the bobbin thread, to rebalance the stitch.

The other important component to smooth stitches and smooth sewing is the needle. Embroidery needles have eyes designed to prevent fine machine-embroidery threads from stripping, shredding, or breaking. Topstitching needles have extra-large eyes and grooves to accommodate heavier threads or multiple threads through the same needle. Metalfil or Metallica needles are the best choice when using metallic embroidery threads.

Choose some sort of linear pattern for your design. It can be as simple as rows of stitches or can be a motif outline that you draw yourself or copy from a pattern book, fabric, or any other source you like.

When embellishing lightweight fabrics or when using dense stitching on any fabric, stabilize the design area first. An embroidery hoop is helpful to frame the design as you sew.

The cuff on this jacket was machine embroidered. To make the looped fringe flower, I sewed two rows of satin stitches using a tailor tacking/faggoting foot and loosening the top tension. Then I added a line of decorative scallop stitches (using a machine-embroidery foot) next to each to secure the loops. Free-motion squiggles accent the buttonhole band.

MATERIALS

Stabilizer, optional (see the sidebar on p. 105)
Embroidery hoop, optional (see the sidebar on p. 105)
Fabric marker
Needle thread, machine embroidery, all-purpose cotton, or polyester
Bobbin thread, all-purpose, bobbin/lingerie, or woolly nylon
Needle, embroidery, topstitching, Metalfil, or Metallica depending on your thread
Machine-embroidery foot

1. Choose the area of the garment you want to embellish, and decide how you want to position the design. Using a fabric marker, mark the design on the right side of the garment. (If you will be following the garment edges or seams, this step is not necessary.)

2. Once you've chosen your threads and needle and placed a machine-embroidery foot on your machine, test the stitch and loosen the tension of the top thread one to two notches.

3. Sew the design by starting at the least conspicuous place. Start and end neatly by using a knot stitch or by sewing in place using a straight stitch.

Using specialty threads in the bobbin

You can expand your options by placing the embroidery thread in the bobbin instead of in the needle. Heavier threads such as pearl cotton, bouclé yarns, and even narrow ribbon that are too thick, wide, or heavy for the needle or the sewing machine give great results if used in the bobbin. You can completely bypass the lower tension, which will allow the thicker threads to feed smoothly.

The best machine stitches for bobbin embroidery are those with long, bold strokes that allow the heavier threads to lie smoothly—these threads are too bulky to use successfully for delicate stitches. Choose bold and simple motifs instead of intricate ones, which are likely to become muddled and crowded if stitched in heavy thread.

Sometimes an imperfect stitch adds character to the overall design. When I tried some chenille yarn in the bobbin, I knew that the yarn was too thick and fuzzy to feed smoothly, so I selected a very long basting stitch to keep the stitch as simple as possible. I hand-wound the bobbin and completely bypassed the bottom tension. As I sewed, the yarn would occasionally gnarl, making little loops instead of a straight line. As it turned out, the gnarls look interesting and work because I intended the chenille to look like a stem on a vine.

To add a simple but "important" embellishment, just wind narrow ribbon onto a bobbin and sew a row of zigzag stitches, being sure to sew with the garment wrong side up so the ribbon is on the right side. To complete the effect on this lined organza blouse, I fringed the collar and hem edges.

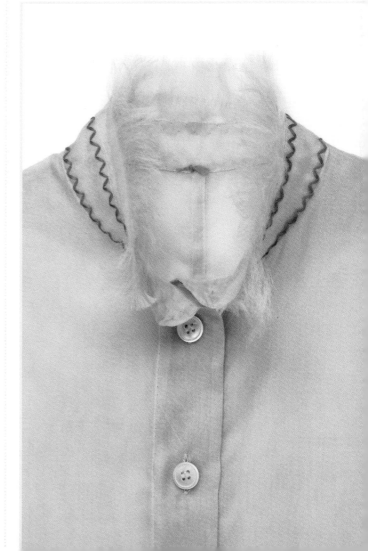

Stabilizer, water soluble or permanent, optional (see the sidebar on p. 105)
Embroidery hoop, optional (see the sidebar on p. 105)
Fabric marker
Bobbin thread, thick and decorative
Needle thread, all-purpose or monofilament
Machine-embroidery foot
Needle, universal point
Large-eyed hand-sewing needle

MACHINE SETTINGS

Needle tension: Standard to loose
Bobbin tension: Loose
Type of stitch: Straight, zigzag, simple decorative, or utility stitch

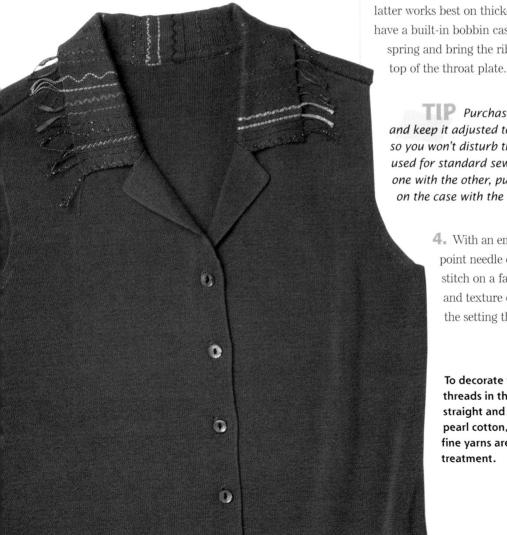

1. Choose the area of the garment you want to embellish, and decide how you want to position the design. Using a fabric marker, mark the design on the wrong side of the garment. Keep in mind that asymmetric designs will be reversed on the right side of the garment.

2. Hand-wind the thread onto the bobbin. Be sure to fill several bobbins so that you can sew with minimal interruptions.

3. Next, thread the top of the machine. If your machine has a removable bobbin case, you have two options: You can loosen the bobbin tension so that the ribbon or cord flows easily through the bobbin case, or you can bypass the tension spring in the case. The latter works best on thicker specialty threads. If you have a built-in bobbin case, just bypass the tension spring and bring the ribbon or cord through to the top of the throat plate.

TIP *Purchase a second bobbin case and keep it adjusted to a loose tension setting so you won't disturb the setting on the case used for standard sewing. To avoid confusing one with the other, put a dot of nail polish on the case with the loosened tension.*

4. With an embroidery foot and universal-point needle on your machine, test the stitch on a fabric similar to the weight and texture of the garment. Write down the setting that you will use.

To decorate this collar, I used specialty threads in the bobbin and a variety of straight and zigzag stitches. Tiny ribbons, pearl cotton, embroidery floss, and fine yarns are all good choices for this treatment.

5. Stitch slowly, following your design line. Be sure to leave long thread tails and ribbon/cord tails at the beginning and end of your work.

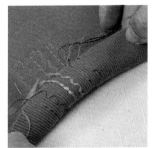

6. Thread the tails onto a large-eyed needle and pass them to the wrong side of the garment, then tie or fasten the ends to the wrong side of the fabric. Cut away the excess.

Free-motion machine stitching

You can create interesting unstructured embroidery designs if you change the presser foot to a darning foot—or use no presser foot at all—and disengage the feed dogs. You really have to experiment with this technique to understand how fun, easy, and flexible it is. You can sew off-road—you don't have to follow a precisely marked pattern and there are no directional restrictions. You can sew curves, zigs, and zags with agility and without stopping to lift the presser foot to pivot. And you don't need a machine that has fancy embroidery stitches.

Free-motion embroidery can be striking or quirky when used alone and can also be very effective when combined with appliqué (see pp. 76–77 for how you can use it to connect or dance across and around the other embellishments with stitches).

To keep things smooth while you sew, use an embroidery hoop or frame the area you're embellishing with your hands. The easiest designs to make are free-form squiggles, curls, and scribbles, but once you get used to the movements you may want to create tighter effects such as outlining or filling in motifs. Here are some tips on free-motion sewing:

- You control the size of the stitch with the sewing speed and by the way you move the hoop. Practice moving the hoop smoothly.

- Sewing at normal speed and moving the hoop quickly yields longer stitches.

- Sewing fast and moving the hoop slowly yields shorter stitches.

I combined free-motion embroidery with structured embroidery stitches and modified utility stitches for this stylized flower.

MATERIALS

Stabilizer, optional (see the sidebar on p. 105)
Embroidery hoop, optional (see the sidebar on p. 105)
Fabric marker
Needle, embroidery, topstitching, Metalfil, or Metallica
Bobbin thread, all-purpose, bobbin/lingerie, or woolly nylon
Needle thread, machine embroidery, all-purpose cotton, or polyester
Darning foot, optional

1. Using a fabric marker, outline the general path that you want to follow on the garment so that you don't end up embroidering over the bust when you mean to embellish the shoulder.

2. Disengage or cover the feed dogs or set the stitch length to 0. Place the portion of the garment to be decorated in an embroidery hoop.

3. Position the hooped fabric under the needle, and bring the bobbin thread to the top of the fabric by rotating the flywheel. Be sure to lower the darning foot (or the presser foot bar if you choose not to use a darning foot) so the thread tension will be even.

Holding both threads, lower the needle into the fabric, then sew a few stitches in place and clip the threads close to the fabric.

4. As you sew, move the hoop so that the fabric passes under the needle in whichever direction you want; move it at a steady pace to keep the stitch length consistent.

5. Once you've finished embellishing, sew a few stitches in place and clip the threads close to the fabric.

Doodle embroidery

Have fun using a plain straight stitch to sew scribbles, doodles, and simple outline designs. The overall effect can look sophisticated, modern, or primitive and definitely whimsical. Use one or more contrasting color threads, and use two ends of thread in the needle (but one in the bobbin) to make the stitching line stand out.

MATERIALS

Tracing paper
Dressmaker's carbon paper, air erasable or white
Stabilizer, permanent
Embroidery hoop, optional
Thread, all-purpose or machine embroidery
Needle, embroidery or topstitching

MACHINE SETTINGS

Needle tension: Loosen one, two, or more increments
Bobbin tension: Standard
Stitch length: 3mm to 3.5mm

1. Start by drawing doodles on tracing paper, then cut them out roughly and pin them onto the garment. Try on the garment to make sure you like the placement.

2. To transfer the doodle designs onto the right side of the garment, insert a sheet of air-erasable or white dressmaker carbon under the tracing paper and use an empty ballpoint pen to draw over the design lines.

Your own doodles or children's drawings can be the basis of easy embroidery embellishments. Simply mark the doodles on the garment, and sew over them with decorative thread in a simple straight stitch.

3. Reinforce the area behind each doodle with stabilizer.

4. Place a marked portion of the garment in an embroidery hoop or frame the fabric with your hands as you sew. Sew over the marked lines; start and end  neatly by sewing in place or using a knot stitch.

5. To finish, either cut the threads or thread the top threads in a needle and pass them to the wrong side of the garment, knot together, and cut off the excess.

TIP If you use two ends of thread in the needle, you can combine two different colors to create just the right shade. When I could not find the perfect vibrant purple, I combined one end of purple with one end of fuchsia to get the color I desired.

Couched Embroidery

Yarns and cords are too thick to feed through either the needle or bobbin of a sewing machine, so if you are tempted to use them for embellishments, you probably think each embroidered motif must be created painstakingly, one stitch at a time, or programmed into an embroidery machine. But if you lay yarns or fine cords on top of a garment in a

TIP If you draw the designs onto the tracing paper using a transfer pencil, you can invert them on the garment and then transfer them by pressing with a warm iron. Keep in mind that the design will be a mirror image of the original—if you have symmetrical motifs, invert the tracing paper drawing and draw the design with the transfer paper.

decorative manner, you can couch (secure) them quickly and easily using your sewing machine. You can arrange the yarn in a linear pattern, with lots of open spaces and meandering details, or coil it tightly to create solid motifs. In both cases, because the yarns are bulkier than sewing threads, the designs will be bold.

Textured yarns such as chenille and bouclé have a tendency to grab the fabric they are being applied to, so they are especially easy to use for this technique. In fact, if you are embellishing a wool garment and the motifs are small, you can probably skip using adhesive and just hold the yarns in place with your fingers while you sew.

Couching small, solid motifs

By tightly coiling a yarn or fine cord or bending it back and forth on itself, you can create small, solid geometric shapes and organic motifs such as simple leaves or buds. To couch each motif to a garment, machine-sew across it in several directions. By using this

I sewed a pretty, looped chenille fringe onto the neckline of this conservative tweed cardigan. I also unraveled some of the fringe and used the yarns to make a small tassel and to coil into dots to couch to the body of the sweater.

technique, you can quickly and completely fill a small motif with yarn—much faster than working a satin stitch by hand. Try making lots of small motifs this way to add an allover pattern to a plain garment. The chenille polka dot design shown in the photo at left was done this way.

This technique is perfect for creating motifs up to 2 in. across. The amount of stitching needed depends upon the size and shape of the motif and the effect you want. The only way to know how much to stitch is by making a sample. Since you don't want the motifs to appear plastered to your garment, less stitching is often better than more.

MATERIALS

Air-erasable fabric marker
Decorative yarn
Temporary spray adhesive
Needle thread, monofilament or all-purpose
*   to match the decorative yarn*
Bobbin thread, all-purpose to match the
*   garment*

1. Using an air-erasable marker, outline the motifs on the right side of the garment. If you want complex motifs, follow steps 1 and 2 of "Doodle Embroidery" on p. 110 to plan and mark them.

2. Arrange the yarn for one motif at a time on the garment. If necessary, use spray adhesive to hold the yarns in place. To form a polka  dot like those on the sweater shown in the photo at left, arrange the yarn in a tight spiral, starting at the center and working

out. (If you are using a nonround motif, start in its center and adjust the coil to conform to its outline.)

3. Secure the yarn by stitching over the design using a straight stitch or a medium zigzag stitch. Sew across the motif several times from perimeter to perimeter, pivoting and changing direction until you've secured the motif with an open grid of stitching. Be sure to start and end neatly by sewing in place or using a knot stitch.

4. To finish, either cut the threads or thread the top threads in a needle and pass them to the wrong side of the garment, knot together, and cut off the excess.

Mock crewel work

This design is derived from my favorite chair, which is upholstered in a traditional hand-embroidered crewel fabric. Knitting yarns are perfect for this project. Wool or wool-like yarns are typically used in crewel embroidery, but you can use any interesting yarn combination that catches your fancy, including chenille or cotton yarn. Since knitting yarns are too thick and fuzzy to be used either in the needle or in the bobbin of a sewing machine, these yarns need to be couched in place to follow the design. To feed the yarns under the needle smoothly, use a braiding foot on your machine.

When selecting yarns, choose a single color that contrasts with your garment or an array as I did for my sweater. You can purchase small skeins of yarn meant for plastic canvas or needlepoint designs at needlework and craft stores.

MATERIALS

Stabilizer, as appropriate
Tracing paper
Dressmaker's carbon paper,
*   air erasable or white*
Decorative yarn
Braiding foot
Needle thread, monofilament
Bobbin thread, all-purpose
*   polyester*
Crewel needle, as
*   appropriate for*
*   the size of*
*   the yarn*

MACHINE SETTINGS

Needle tension: Loosen
*   two increments*
Bobbin tension: Standard
Stitch: Medium zigzag,
*   3mm wide and long*

1. Reinforce the area behind the design areas with the stabilizer.

2. Draw the motifs on tracing paper and cut them out roughly. Then pin them onto the garment to see where they'll look best. Try on the garment to make sure you like the overall look.

3. To transfer the crewel designs onto the right side of the garment, insert a sheet of air-erasable or white

Wallpapers, rugs, and fabrics offer a great source of embroidery motifs. This design is adapted from one of my favorite chairs, which is covered with embroidered crewel fabric.

dressmaker carbon under the tracing paper and use an empty ballpoint pen to draw over the design lines (see the bottom photo at right on p. 110).

TIP *If you are embellishing a light-weight knit and using a knit stabilizer, orient the stabilizer so its direction of greatest stretch runs vertically on the sweater.*

4. Next, position a marked portion of the garment at your sewing machine. Choose the yarn for the first part of your design, and lay it over the marked outline, leaving a 6-in. tail extending behind the needle. Lower the braiding foot, centering the yarn under the groove, and secure the yarn to the garment by zigzag-stitching over it. As you sew, frame the fabric with you hands, stopping as needed to guide the yarn along the marked outline with your fingers.

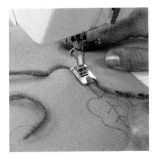

5. Once you have finished with the first color, leave a 6-in. tail and cut off the remainder. Look at the stitches to make sure they are not distorting the garment. It may be necessary to redistribute the couched yarn by pulling it gently under the zigzag stitches so both design and garment lie flat.

6. Repeat steps 4 and 5 until you've couched the entire design, changing colors as desired. To end, thread the yarns and top threads in the crewel needle and pass them to the wrong side of the garment. Tie them together or hand-sew to the back side of the garment and cut off the excess.

Satin-Stitch Openings

In the first part of this chapter, I've shown ways to embellish clothing with surface embroidery. In the following section, I combine easy machine satin stitching with slashes and cutouts for a completely different twist on thread embellishments.

Buttonhole basketweave

Functional buttonholes become very decorative if you place them side-by-side in rows and lace interesting trims through them to create a basketweave pattern. This is a great way to add a tailored embellishment to the area parallel to the hemline, to one side of a jacket front, or even to the edge of a collar. If you've had less than stellar results making buttonholes on your machine, you can breathe a sigh of relief—in this instance the trims woven through them will mask any imperfections.

By using this easy and straightforward technique, you can create a variety of effects by varying the size and spacing of the buttonholes. If you orient them vertically, the woven pattern will be horizontal—and horizontal buttonholes will create a vertical weave. If you sew the buttonholes at consistent intervals, making the space between them equal to the buttonhole length as I did for the skirt shown in the photo on p. 116, you'll get an even basketweave. Sew them in spaced pairs, and you'll have an uneven weave. The more varied the spacing, the less regular the weave.

Try making several rows of buttonholes, changing the buttonhole length on each row to accommodate trims of different widths. If you place the buttonholes end-to-end instead of side-by-side and then lace a soft, wide trim through them, the woven effect will be soft and puffed.

Buttonholes are good for much more than fastenings—I like to sew them in rows and then weave contrasting bands of fabric or ribbon through them. Place them strategically above a hem or parallel to a front opening.

For weaving you can use ribbon, bias-cut fabric, horsehair braid, decorative cording, strips of Ultrasuede, or anything lightweight and flexible that can be laundered in a manner appropriate for the garment. Your choice of contrasting or matching thread for the buttonholes also contributes to the final design.

MATERIALS

Stabilizer, permanent
Air-erasable marker or
*   tailor's chalk*
Thread, all-purpose
Buttonhole foot
Trim for weaving

1. On fabric similar in weight to your garment, sew and cut open a sample buttonhole to be sure the length is adequate. For woven trim to lie smoothly, the buttonholes must each be a little longer than the trim is wide.

2. Choose the area of the garment you want to embellish, then decide how you want to position the buttonholes and how much to space them. To help you visualize the effect, mark and slash a piece of paper or scrap fabric, weave your trim through the openings, then hold or pin this mockup over the garment.

Plan your pattern so the ends of the woven trim will be hidden on the wrong side of the garment—unless you prefer to see them on the right side. If the pattern goes all around the garment, be sure it repeats appropriately.

3. Reinforce the wrong side of the buttonhole area with stabilizer.

4. Using an air-erasable marker, mark the buttonhole placement on your garment. Sew the buttonholes and cut them open.

TIP *A quick way to cut the buttonholes is by placing each on a cutting mat and carefully slashing it using a craft knife.*

5. Weave the trim in and out through the openings.

6. At each end, secure the trim to the garment by sewing a line of straight stitches next to the outside edge of the buttonhole satin stitch.

Cutwork

Cutwork is a form of embroidery in which a linear design is first "drawn" with straight stitches, then enclosed portions of the design are cut out, and finally the design is redrawn with satin stitches so that each opening is framed and the cut edges are secured by stitches. Traditional cutwork is done by hand, but it is easy to do by machine. The satin stitches can match or contrast the garment, as you wish.

DESIGNER IDEA

Try the following variations to create different basketweave effects.

- *Emphasize a scoop neckline by sewing one or more rows of buttonholes, then weaving in trim. Use narrow (less than ½ in.) and flexible trims so they conform to the neckline curve. Space a pair of buttonholes equidistant from the center front and another pair equidistant from the center back—if the interval doesn't repeat evenly around the neckline, cheat at the shoulders.*

- *Weave wide trims through small buttonholes so the buttonholes pinch the trim and create a scalloped effect. The trim must be bias cut, soft, and flexible in order to conform to the openings.*

- *Use colorful or contrasting thread to sew huge vertical buttonholes along the lower edge of a skirt or top. The buttonholes should be 2 in., 4 in., 6 in., or 8 in. long. Select different lengths and position the buttonholes so that you have an up-and-down staggered effect, then cut the buttonholes open.*

The designs can be geometric or curvilinear, quite simple or very elaborate. Whichever you choose, keep the cutouts fairly small so they don't lose their shape. Bear in mind that the more closely the cutouts are spaced, the more prone they are to distortion. Sometimes it's difficult to tell if the motif will hold its shape, so make a sample in a fabric similar to your garment to give you the answer—and let you get the hang of the technique.

You can create any design you like, but if you are unfamiliar with this technique, I suggest you start with something very simple, such as the isolated square openings around the neckline of the dress shown in the photo on p. 118. These are easy to do because you don't have to mark out a complex design or figure out the path to follow when sewing. You can simply make a cardboard template for the opening, place it on the garment wherever you like, draw around it, reposition it, and draw again. Then you satin stitch each marked outline. Readymade stencils are a good option for templates if you want something more complex than a simple geometric shape but don't want to make your own.

I like to use cutwork designs along areas of the garment that are already stable and have facings, such as necklines. When you add cutwork to soft areas, you must reinforce them with stabilizer as you would for any embroidery technique.

The over-edge foot and satin-edge foot are two special presser feet that will make the stitching even easier to do; use one of them if you can. They work by forming the satin stitches over a supporting finger that prevents the thread from squeezing and distorting the cut edge of the fabric. If you don't have either of these feet, use an embroidery foot.

MATERIALS

Stabilizer, fusible permanent or cutaway
Template or stencil
Air-erasable marker or tailor's chalk
Thread, machine embroidery or all-purpose
Needle, embroidery or universal point
Presser feet, standard and satin edge, over edge, or embroidery

MACHINE SETTINGS

Needle tension: Loosen 1 to 2 settings
Bobbin tension: Standard
Stitches: Short straight, 1.5mm to 2mm long; narrow zigzag; satin stitch, 2mm wide or wider

1. Choose the area of the garment you want to embellish, and decide how you want to position the design. Reinforce the wrong side of the design area with stabilizer.

I like to use simple machine satin stitching to create a cutwork border along a neckline, front edge, or hemline. Even something as straightforward as a pattern of rectangles will add snap to a plain garment.

SEWING INSIDE CORNERS FOR CUTWORK

It's a little tricky to sew satin stitches around the inside corners of cutout areas. Here's a method that works for me.

Beginning at one corner, sew satin stitches along the edge of the opening toward the next corner, sewing up to and then one or two stitches beyond the stitches reinforcing the next edge. Adjust the machine to a very short straight stitch and raise the presser foot. If the needle is down, rotate the fly-  wheel to raise it out of the fabric, and pull the fabric and satin stitch back just enough to free the satin stitches from the stitch finger.

Next, rotate the flywheel to insert the needle in the fabric again, then pivot the garment so you are ready to sew the next edge of the cutout. (The reason for switching to a straight stitch before pivoting is to keep the thread to the left of the stitch finger and to prevent thread loops from forming after you pull back the fabric.) After pivoting, adjust the machine back to the satin stitch and check that the garment is positioned so that the satin stitch aligns with the edge of the opening. Continue to satin-stitch around the opening in this manner.

2. Place the template on the right side of the garment, and draw around it using the fabric marker. You can reposition the template as many times as desired, drawing around it each time.

3. Next, sew along the design lines using a standard presser foot and a short straight stitch. If the fabric frays easily, sew a narrow zigzag stitch instead of straight stitches to stabilize the edge and prevent whiskers of unruly threads from peeking through the final satin stitches.

4. Cut out the garment fabric and any stabilizer inside each motif, being sure to cut just inside the stitches.

5. Place an over-edge, satin-edge, or machine-embroidery foot on your machine, then sew around each opening using a satin stitch and stitching over the cut edge of the fabric. Start and end neatly by using a knot stitch or by sewing in place.

Sources

Atlanta Thread and Supply Co.
695 Red Oak Rd.
Stockbridge, GA 30282
(800) 847-1001
Threads, eyelets, grommets, and tools

Beyond Beadery
P.O. Box 460
Rollinsville, CO 80474
(800) 840-5548
Fax: (303) 258-9394
www.beyondbeadery.com
Beads and beading supplies

Clotilde
B3000
Louisiana, MO 63353-3000
(800) 772-2891
www.clotilde.com
Threads and notions

Jo-Ann Etc., Jo-Ann Fabrics
Hundreds of fabric/craft stores across the country
www.joann.com
Fabrics, beads, and threads

M&J Trimming
1008 Avenue of the Americas
New York, NY 10018
(212) 842-5000
www.mjtrim.com
Every kind of trim

Meissner Sewing Center
2417 Cormorant Way
Sacramento, CA 95815
(800) 920-2202; (916) 920-2121
Threads, decorative braids, and decorative yarns

Michael's Crafts
(800) 642-4235
Yarns, beads, and trinkets

Nancy's Notions
P.O. Box 683
Beaver Dam, WI 53916-0683
(800) 833-0690; (920) 887-0391
www.nancysnotions.com
Threads and notions

Rio Grande
(800) 443-6766 (USA); (800) 253-9738 (Canada)
Fax: (800) 645-4850
www.riogrande.com
Beads and supplies

York Beads
10 W. 37th St.
New York, NY 10018
(800) 223-6676; (212) 594-7040
Beads and supplies

Index

Note: page references in *italics* indicate a photograph or illustration.